BORN GUILTY

BORN GUILTY

Children of Nazi Families

PETER SICHROVSKY

Translated by Jean Steinberg

Basic Books, Inc., Publishers   *New York*

Library of Congress Cataloging-in-Publication Data

Schuldig geboren. English.
  Born guilty.
  Translation of: Schuldig geboren.
  1. National socialism—Psychological aspects.
2. Children—Germany—History—20th century. 3. Children
—Austria—History—20th century. 4. Guilt. I. Steinberg,
Jean, 1918– . II. Sichrovsky, Peter,
1947– . III. Title.
DD256.5.S34413 1988   943′.0088054   87–47773
ISBN 0–465–00742–2

English translation, copyright © 1988 by Basic Books, Inc.
Originally published in German as
Schuldig geboren: Kinder aus Nazifamilien
© 1987 by Verlag Kiepenheuer & Witsch, Köln
Printed in the United States of America
Designed by Vincent Torre
88 89 90 91 RRD 9 8 7 6 5 4 3 2 1

CONTENTS

BORN GUILTY

Introduction

MY RECENT BOOK about young Jews in Germany and Austria grew out of a compelling personal interest. This time I have no such motivation. This book deals with "the others."

Nonetheless, these "others" are not strangers. I grew up among them, with these children of the Nazis. I played with their sons and dated their daughters. We all went to the same schools and probably sat next to each other. Born in 1947 to Jewish emigrants who had returned to Vienna, I was surrounded by children whose parents only yesterday had wanted to murder my parents. Given the small number of Jews living in Vienna after World War II, and the vast number of Nazis in Vienna before and after the war, it is a mathematical probability that in my childhood and adolescence I was surrounded by the children of fervent believers.

However, in retrospect, that subject never came up between us. The children wrapped their parents' past in silence, not necessarily consciously, but apparently they were unable to talk about something they had never been told.

These "others" were not strangers, yet they were alien to me. In the course of my interviews I found that I had been living alongside them, rather than with them.

As regards the parents of my Jewish friends, I was familiar with their past: I knew how and where they had survived. But the history of the parents of those "others" was a mystery. I cannot recall a single conversation with a fellow student in which the role of his parents during the Nazi period was ever alluded to. My reaction to this memory hole was to tell them about the fate of my parents, the drama of my grandparents, as though wanting to establish as unambiguously as possible that my story was unlike that of the majority of the people living here.

The only time the subject was broached was by a German student I met in London. We happened to be staying at the same hotel, and we fell in love. One evening while dancing to the Beatles I suddenly yelled into her ear—the music was very loud—that here we were dancing together while our fathers probably had tried to kill each other. She didn't understand what I meant, and so I explained that my father had fled from Vienna to London in 1938 and had served in the British army.

That put an end to the fun and to whatever plans I'd had for that evening. Edda, that was her name, returned to our table, sat down, and told me that her father had been in the SS. Again and again she asked me about my parents, about their lives in emigration, but she couldn't tell me anything about her father's life during those years. All she knew was that he'd been a member of the SS. She knew neither his rank nor his function.

My preoccupation with the children of the active participants in the deeds of the Third Reich thus was a venture into familiar territory inhabited, as I was to learn, by unfamiliar women and men. I knew little about their cares, their fantasies and problems, which were a burden they carried around with them because of their parents' past.

When I began working on this book I thought about which of two possible approaches to the children of Nazis would be the most promising. Should I get in touch with the children of well-known Nazis, or should I ask around for the names of children of Nazi families? The first approach seemed more direct. One contact led to another, and before long I was in touch, either in person or by phone, with about twenty-five women and men whose fathers might be considered representative figures of the National Socialist era.

Many declined to be interviewed, some because they had built new lives for themselves and wanted to forget the past, some because they feared they would be asked to criticize their fathers, and still others because they simply wished to be left alone. Among those who refused to talk to me was the daughter of Hermann Göring, although I later read an interview with her in a magazine. Not all who agreed to an interview appear in these pages. What I was after was a mixture of important personages and simple fellow travelers. To limit the book to children of well-known Nazis would have given it a nuance I hoped to avoid. After all, the Third Reich was not made up solely of leaders. On the contrary. It was the vast mass of loyal, decent bureaucrats—policemen, officers, mayors, railroad employees, teachers, and so on—that greased the wheels of the Nazi dictatorship. These were the people that interested me. I wanted to know their children: how they grew up, what they knew, what questions they asked, and how they managed to live with what they knew.

In the case of lower-level Nazis I depended on leads furnished by friends and acquaintances. This put me in touch with a group of people who voluntarily referred to their parents as Nazis. Because the children, not the perpetrators, were to be my subject, I did not focus on the deeds of the parents. I was interested in the opinion of the children, whether or not they saw their fathers or mothers as Nazis. I never spoke to any of the parents. The most important criterion was the children's assessment of their parents, how they saw them.

This book does not offer a hierarchy of horrors. The child of someone responsible for the deaths of thousands is not necessarily of greater interest than the child of a small-town mayor who may have merely put some Social Democrats in jail.

When I first approached the children of some not particularly prominent Nazis I made some crucial mistakes. They rebuffed me because they sensed a critical attitude. Formulations that I had thought noncommittal, such as "Wasn't your father a well-known SS officer?" or "Aren't you the son of a prominent Nazi?" were reason enough for many to change their minds about the interview.

I learned that I had to revise the wording of my questions. After that initial experience I would refer to fathers who had been "active during the Nazi era," or who had been "politically engaged." In some cases I even went so far as to offer the interview as a means to refute the charges against their fathers.

The book that resulted is a mixture of interviews with children of the famous and not-so-famous, with men and women who hate their parents or continue to admire them, who think of their parents as murderers or as heroes or as ordinary people, parents like any others. I have made no attempt to categorize or group the children of Nazis, let alone interpret them on the basis of their attitudes. I leave that to the experts. My compilation does not claim to be a scientific sample. It is an arbitrary mixture of the lives of some people in present-day Germany and Austria. Among the forty people I interviewed I found a wide range of responses to the actions of the parents. Yet despite all the differences, I also found a number of similarities.

Perhaps the greatest insight I gained was the fact that the members of the postwar generation had never had the experience of seeing their parents in their heroic Nazi roles. The radiant youthful hero in SS uniform, firm in his belief in Hitler and final victory, belongs to history. His children know him only from pictures and books. Born toward the end of the war or afterward, they have no such memories of their parents. Fleeing advancing armies, bombed out, homeless and unemployed, hiding from the Allied police, arrested and jailed, these parents are remembered by their children as victims of the war, as victims of a lost war.

One woman described her father, a high-ranking SS officer occupying an important post in a concentration camp, as a "nervous, trembling man, in constant fear that the police would get him. Four of us were living in a single room, my father had no work, and was afraid to go out in daytime. Is that what power-hungry monsters responsible for the deaths of millions look like?" she asked. "I could never see my father in that role."

The children of the Nazis never experienced their fathers in an active role, except possibly within the confines of the family. The parents saw themselves as victims, and when they were young the children accepted that view. However, once they became old enough to learn something about the actual role their parents played during the war, the children themselves often became victims—the victims of their parents. Many of the people I interviewed saw themselves in that light, as the victims of a mentality which, even though the war had been lost, fostered a fascistic attitude in the home. The external setting had changed; Germany and Austria had long since become democratic states. But the National Socialist ideology was deeply embedded in the minds of the perpetrators and their henchmen, and so the postwar generation found itself confronted by democratic structures on the outside and fascistic family structures at home.

The following letter from the father of a young Austrian musician to his son, who had fallen in love with a Jewish woman, is a telling example.

Linz, Tuesday, April 6, 1965

My dear Herwig!

There is a reason why I am writing you today. On Friday Ina is going to return to Frankfurt. The days that follow won't be very easy for you. Perhaps you will find it reassuring to know that your problems are shared by me, and that I am judging your situation not only with my heart but also with a clear head. Not only the situation as it appears at this moment, but also the one that might arise. I am urging you to say goodbye in a friendly but noncommittal fashion, and in doing so mention that a written communication will follow. Put off everything still unresolved, all problems, agreements, etc., until a later date. Leave everything open. I'm giving you this advice for tactical reasons. Now to the matter itself, something you and I should talk about frankly.

Much has happened between Ina and you, but also in connection with us. There is much that could be said, criticized, advised, compared, etc. Your mother and I agree when we say that many of Ina's shortcomings could in time be overcome, smoothed over. We also know that you have made a number of mistakes. All this would be grounds for discussion and advice. But now the problem of Ina's heritage has added a catastrophic element. Today I see many things very differently. This problem must be looked at from two completely different vantage points. First the personal one: very regrettable, of course. Ina is not responsible for that. As far as Ina is concerned, this problem must be tackled very tactfully, best of all even ignored for the time being, unless she herself forces us to change our mind and attitude. Out of personal compassionate understanding I agreed to receive and treat Ina politely. I would also like to take Ina to the station on Friday. This ought to tell you something about my objective attitude. To formulate this attitude clearly and unequivocally: your decision is and remains entirely your own, as does mine, which is that my door shall remain closed to Ina once she leaves here.

This dry communication may seem very harsh. But there are two reasons for it. The first rests on the fact that under no circumstances am I prepared to change my basic attitude toward life. The second has to do with you yourself: I know that in the long run, despite your best intentions, you are not capable of bearing up under what is bound to be a psychologically crushing burden. Perhaps not everyone in your world would greet you with reservations and prejudice, but perhaps you would see reservations where none exist. It is my absolute duty as your father to call the consequences to your attention and to tell you without beating about the bush what to expect if you bring someone of Jewish descent into our clan. I have to tell you this, as harsh as it may sound, and in fact is.

I am giving you time and advise you to give yourself time before making a final decision. Should you decide that this episode has been closed for good, then tell me so. I would also like to call to your attention something that doesn't necessarily have to be so, and I even hope that it won't come to pass— namely, the possibility of legal consequences, which cannot be ruled out. I therefore ask you not to expose yourself in any way. When the first letters are exchanged let me know, lest either out of rashness or ignorance of the situation you put things on paper that might harm you. Since you'll be here for the weekend, we will have a chance to talk about it. Be nice now and don't be rough on Ina. Her situation isn't an enviable one either. But be careful. Don't even mention the word marriage. If push comes to shove you might find yourself dealing with forces that you with your ideas and opinions are absolutely and completely unequipped for.

I therefore ask you to understand my concern; it is the concern of a father for his son.

Regards and love,
Your father

As far as the neighbors are concerned all they have to know is that your *Visitor* is leaving to continue her studies. Other than that not a single word to anyone!!

Many years later the son ran into Ina at a concert and told her of his conflict with his parents. She told him that she wasn't Jewish, that he apparently had misunderstood something she had said. But it was that "misunderstanding" that gave the son the liberating strength to leave home. Now he is a musician working primarily with groups playing traditional Jewish music.

The reaction to the feeling of victimization by one's own parents varies from person to person. Many see themselves as sufferers. Thus a twenty-nine-year-old student, the son of a concentration camp guard, referred to himself as the Jew of his family. Using the victims of National Socialism as props, searching for reasons for persecution within oneself, reasons which in bygone days would have relegated them to the ranks of the persecuted, is not an unusual reaction of these children to the culpability of their parents.

Those feelings are often intensified when these children of Nazis talk among themselves about their fate. In answer to my question whether they spoke differently among themselves than they did to me, a forty-year-old psychologist told me that I wanted to deny her the role of victim. When she talks about this subject with friends she is talking to fellow victims, but when she is talking to me she is reminded of her possible complicity in the crime.

Another typical reaction is protectiveness of the father. Even when the evidence was indisputable, some of the interviewees reacted vehemently and said they were not about to revile their fathers. Some sought to trivialize the deeds of their fathers, saying they had been small fry or had served in an area where there had not been any concentration camps. Others said that their parents were very ordinary people who had behaved no worse than any other parents, had never abused them, and they therefore saw no reason to distance themselves from them or to judge them. What mattered to them was how their parents treated them, not what they had done in the past.

INTRODUCTION

All the people I talked to knew that I was a Jew. I mentioned this fact at the very outset, and I never felt that it engendered any reluctance on their part. However, in the course of the interviews they would refer to the fact of my Jewishness. Most of the time they tried to explain to me that because of my relationship to my parents, which undoubtedly was different from theirs, I could not understand what growing up with Nazi parents was like. Occasionally this took the form of almost aggressive attacks and accusations that in my situation, despite the sufferings of my family, I had had an easier time of it than they, the sons and daughters of murderers. I had to agree. The crucial difference between the children of the victims and the children of the perpetrators is that the former do not have to live with the fear and suspicions of what their parents had done during the war.

What also interested me about my project was the scientific investigation of this phenomenon. Annette Hahn, a young Munich physician, undertook a study of the psychological and psychiatric literature on this subject in German scientific archives and libraries. Her quest ended within days. At most, twenty papers on the psychological problems of the children of Nazis are to be found in the archives of the Federal Republic. The psychologists who proliferated during the 1960s and 1970s valiantly labored to make the Germans happy and serene—and to help them forget their own history. From collective barbarism to collective amnesia. A university professor was asked why so little attention was being paid in Germany to the effects of the deeds of the fathers on their children. He said that it was not a popular subject. But some of these children undoubtedly sought treatment. Among the thousands who grew up in the households of unreconciled Nazis and who sought the help of psychologists or psychiatrists, that phenomenon must have been recognized as the cause of psychic trauma. How did all those "helpers" treat this subject? What did they do with these patients? How could they help if their training and scientific work excluded this central concern?

Perhaps it is already too late. By now the grandchildren of the perpetrators are of college age, and their parents were deprived of the opportunity to learn from the history of their own parents. The silence of the perpetrators can become a time bomb. An entire generation, a generation torn between the reality of an external new democracy and old fascistic family ideals, failed to assimilate the past, and because of this failure it could not forge a new identity, one that would make a recurrence of the past unimaginable. Nearly all of the people I interviewed, regardless of their attitude toward their parents, were convinced that what happened under the Nazis could recur. Their mistrust, their awareness of the traces of the past among their compatriots, coupled with the fear of such a repetition, has not made the children of the perpetrators particularly optimistic citizens.

Not only are the children faced with the inability to right the wrongs of their parents, but they also lack the essential positive identification with their parents. These children were traumatized by the coldness and silence of the parental generation, and if they managed to master the past at all, they did so only with great effort. The much-discussed "inability to mourn"—the parents didn't even mourn for their beloved Führer—typified the mood of the families after the war. The children's view of their parents as "victims" of the war reflects the reality of the children's experience. Those great heroes, the masters and supermen, turned into puny figures who saw themselves as the victims of misfortune, never as the instigators of disaster. Personal guilt and responsibility, let alone shame on the part of the parents, were hardly ever mentioned. The generation of the perpetrators treated their children to lies, silence, and dishonesty. "If my mother even once had said to me that she was a participant," a woman told me in the course of our interview, "that she had made a terrible mistake, that she hoped I, her daughter, would learn from it, I could have become reconciled to her, even if it turned out that she had been a concentration camp guard."

The silence of the parents coupled with the persistence of fascistic attitudes within the family colors the history of the children. So if they see themselves as victims of their Nazi parents, they are not altogether unrealistic.

Many of the children of these Nazis have taken over their parents' role of suffering. This becomes apparent particularly during discussions touching on social and political problems, when disagreements with governmental authorities or political adversaries are seen in terms of the Nazi era. Some liken the Greens to the Nazis and others liken the police to the Gestapo, but in either case there is an attempt to dramatize the situation by comparing the adversary to the Nazis and seeing oneself as the victim.

The biggest failure of the perpetrators is their failure to bear witness. The ugliest among them frequently turn into whining Germans who cannot understand why after all these years they are still looked upon as being responsible for the horrors of the Nazi era. With so much evil in the world, be it the Russians or the Americans, they ask, isn't it time to let bygones be bygones?

Today more talk in the Federal Republic centers on whether history has known tragedies comparable to Auschwitz rather than on how this could have happened in a Christian, civilized country like Germany. Politicians openly state that they, as young officers in 1945, did not feel that they had been liberated, but rather that they had been vanquished, and there is a running debate about monuments to honor all the casualties of the Third Reich as victims of the war, regardless of whether they were murderers or murder victims.

This talk of the innocently vanquished is now supposed to form the basis for a new democratic orientation. Those "old" Germans certainly have not made it easy for the "new" Germans. They shoved things under the rug until the pile of dirt grew so big that one trips over it. In this book we hear from a generation that continues to trip—over their parents' past, over their cowardly failure to talk about this past, over their failure to admit their guilt. Whether this stumbling gait can be converted into a firm step remains to be seen.

1

Anna

The Decent One

MY LIFE can be summed up in just a few sentences. Born 1947 in Munich. Childhood in Munich. School in Munich. Nursing school. Married at twenty-eight. Housewife. Mother of two children. My husband works in a bank. He takes care of us and I take care of the household. We're well off.

This part of my story is easy. It can perhaps be summed up as follows: When I was thirteen I found out that my father had not, as I'd been told by my mother, been a combat soldier during the war, but that he'd worked in a concentration camp. And that my mother, also contrary to what she'd told me, hadn't been sitting at home worrying, waiting for news from her husband at the front. No, my father came home every evening, like a man returning from the office. Sat down at the table and ate the meal

The Decent One

Mother had prepared for her hard-working spouse. He did his job, and she hers.

When I was still young—I remember it like today, it was in 1959—a letter arrived at the house which changed everything, absolutely everything. But it also left everything as before. I know that sounds contradictory, but that's how it was. However important and weighty that event, it basically changed nothing.

Apparently charges had been brought against my father by former prisoners. You can imagine what went on in our family when that happened. But maybe you with your history can't imagine it. At the time my father was working for the police. He got the job soon after the war. He had his work, we were well off; we were like any other ordinary family. Perhaps we were even happy, I don't know. At least I don't remember being a particularly unhappy child. Fascism? Nazis? Persecution of Jews? That whole business was never mentioned in our house.

"During the war your father fought at the front, like all other men," my mother used to tell me. And I wasn't supposed to ask him about it because it upset him too much. And I didn't ask him. Why should I have? War? That happened long before my time. True, there were all those bombed-out houses in the city, but everything else was just stories, things that had happened to others.

But then came that letter. I don't remember whether it was from the government or from a lawyer; I have no idea. And I never read it. One evening, a few days after the letter arrived, my father didn't come home. I was sitting in the kitchen with my mother eating supper. I sensed that something was wrong. For days hardly a word had been spoken in my presence. My parents walked around with worried faces. My mother even had tears in her eyes. Today I am surprised at myself for not having asked any questions. I saw everything, heard everything, but paid no attention, lived my little life as a schoolgirl, and told myself that Mother will tell me if it's something I ought to know. Of course I knew that something had happened. Father was on the phone all the time and didn't go to work. Every evening men with important-looking briefcases came to the house. The only thing that really upset me at the time was that these men always had their meetings in the living room, which meant that I couldn't watch TV.

One evening I was sitting with Mother in the kitchen having my supper when she raised her head, looked at me, and said: "Anna, you're now old enough for me to have a talk with you." I put down my spoon, looked at her, listened to her, and didn't understand a word of what she was saying. She seemed almost ridiculous to me, and even today I remember that evening as being rather curious. For the first time my mother seemed unsure. She began to stammer, excited and hysterical; it was a confused account interspersed with sobs and these recurrent phrases: "If anyone should ask you about your father, you know nothing. And if they ask you what your parents have told you about the war, you tell them nothing. Do you understand what I'm saying to you? Regardless of who asks you, you know nothing." Then she tried to explain something to me, talked of false reports, of denunciations, of evil people who wanted to take our father away from us. I didn't understand a word. And since I wasn't in the habit of asking questions, I was satisfied with the admonition to say nothing. What could I have told, anyway?

My mother was terribly afraid. At least that's how I see it today. Afraid of everything: me, the police, the trial, the neighbors, and undoubtedly also the survivors.

Life at home became increasingly disorganized. Every evening some men would show up and sit with Father; Mother usually stayed in the kitchen, tearful, and every now and then she'd serve them coffee or beer. I couldn't talk to my father at all. He stopped going to work, spent the whole day at home, hardly saying a word. I stayed out of his way, avoided any contact with him—and strange as this may seem, slowly began to move away from my parents.

This went on for a whole year, until the next dramatic incident. I had meanwhile turned thirteen and become a little more grown-up. I began to fight with my parents about ridiculous minor things, though they seemed very important to me at the time—like refusing to wear what my mother had laid out for me or going for a walk with my girlfriend, the kind of things my own children do without giving it a thought.

One afternoon, shortly before the summer vacation, the telephone rang. My parents had been even more nervous than before. My mother had been sitting next to the phone waiting for it to ring. It did; she picked up the receiver, and except for "yes, yes," her voice growing firmer with each yes, she said nothing. Then she hung up the phone and with tears in her eyes came over to me, embraced me, and said: "Now everything is all right again. They weren't able to hurt your father. Everything is fine again."

Now came my question, the first real question I had ever asked my mother. You can laugh at me if you want, or refuse to believe me, or think I must have been retarded, but that was the first time I asked, "Mother, what's all right again?" And my mother said to me: "Your father has been acquitted; he is not guilty. He's never been guilty."

These words and my mother's reaction were like a vehicle transporting me into another stage of my life. Nervously and somewhat irritated I asked her what he'd been acquitted of, what he'd done, who had brought charges against him, why charges had been brought. Needless to say, my mother didn't tell me anything. She talked in circles, spoke words whose meaning I knew: shameless, denunciation, governmental terror, and— don't get upset—the Jews. That was the first time that word was spoken in our house. Never before had my parents said anything about Jews; it was a word that didn't exist.

That conversation put an end to my naïveté and childish stupidity. I began to be suspicious. For the first time I began to sense that something was being kept from me.

Father returned home an hour later with some of his friends. All of them were slightly tipsy. They were flushed, laughed a lot, and embraced and kissed me. I was disgusted. Then beer was ordered by the barrel in celebration of his acquittal. The whole thing is so terrible when I think about it now. I don't feel that I can judge him, let alone condemn him. I don't want to talk about what he'd done during the war. Perhaps they threatened him or put pressure on him. Who knows what I would have done at the time? But why celebrate now? Why act as though the home team had scored a big win? I'm not exaggerating when I tell you that that was the worst evening of my life. And still worse are my memories today, now that I know why my father was brought to trial.

After a few days things returned to normal. My father went back to work; my mother went back to cleaning, cooking, and shopping, and I continued to go to school. But I developed a passionate urge to get to the bottom of their secret. My parents weren't about to tell me anything. And I simply didn't understand the many remarks and allusions, the cynical references by neighbors, schoolmates, and even some teachers. After all, I knew for a fact that my father had been a soldier in the war like everyone else. But two weeks later I knew better.

Today it's easy to say this. And it also sounds so pathetic. How often have I talked about it with my husband. But what is the most important event in a person's life? Mine undoubtedly was the discovery that my father had been head of a guard detachment in a concentration camp and that he'd been accused of murder. I found out about it. And what happened then? Do you think that my discovery changed anything? Should I have run away from home? Or drawn up a private indictment against a mother and a father who for years had lied to their child? They had fed me, clothed me, and at Christmas there was a tree and presents. Do I do any more for my children? A father who was a murderer. What does that sound like? My life wasn't like a Dostoevsky novel. Mine weren't the right type of heroes.

We had a teacher at our school who was a little older than the rest, a friendly, kind man. Regardless of how we behaved in class, he always remained calm. We didn't take him very seriously. But one day after class he took me aside—most of the other kids had already left—and quietly said to me: "Anna, if you should ever feel like talking to someone, particularly because of that business with your father, you can come to me. I will try to help you."

Nobody had ever said that to me. After only a few days I took him up on his offer. He invited me to his house. That in itself was unusual. Why did he do it? I don't know. I never asked him. I went to him the next day, and the day after that, and again the day after that. I'm still in touch with him. He is now almost eighty. We never talk about my father. He is a sort of grandfather, and probably also a father substitute. He is such an uncomplicated, solid man. Everything he says is right. I believe every word, and I accept his advice like that of my doctor.

What did he tell me at the time? What could he tell me? Who can imagine a thirteen-year-old girl stupid enough never to have heard of the horrors of concentration camps and naïve enough to believe everything her parents told her? The first shock was to find out what had happened; the second, to find out that my father had played a part in it. Of course I knew that there had been concentration camps and that 6 million Jews had been murdered. We'd been told about it in school. But I had also been told fairy tales in school, stories like Little Red Riding Hood. And we learned about the Crusades and later, when I was older, about the French Revolution. And still later, about World War II and the gas chambers. But who, for God's sake, had ever told us that our own parents had been there? Or that thousands were executed during the French Revolution? Yes, I remember our history teacher's dramatic depiction of the misdeeds of Robespierre. But who could believe that the baker next door or the English teacher or that nice policeman who stopped the cars at the school crossing or the man at the passport office participated in the murders during the war? And one's own father!

The history class and all those other accounts were stories about events in the past. We were such nice, cheerful children, with our neat skirts and hair ribbons. Sundays my father carried me on his shoulders as we walked in the woods. My parents and I played catch, and the one who dropped the ball would be penalized. Silly, harmless pastimes. Solid and decent to a fare-thee-well.

There were no casualties, no wars, no threats. There was no mourning. That's how it was. Nobody mourned in my family. Nobody had died in the war. My father's brothers survived, and my grandfathers were too old for military service. Nor had any family member died in bombing raids. But maybe that wasn't the reason they didn't mourn.

And then came that afternoon with Horst. That's what I call that teacher now. He himself had been in a camp as a Communist. He wasn't a big shot, and so he was left alone for a long time. But a few months before the end of the war they picked him up, a last round-up of prisoners before that last push to make sure that the final victory wouldn't be endangered. Horst didn't say much about what happened to him. I think he was much more concerned about what the other people—like my father —had done. I don't want to go into details about the things he told me. The most important thing I learned from him was that the cruelties in Germany had taken place not in some remote past but just before I was born. And that the generation that had caused, instigated, and thus also committed those acts was not only living, but living in my neighborhood. And that my own father had been an active participant in the crimes.

Horst was forever talking about his duty to tell me about the past. In that respect he was like my father; he, too, loved to talk about duty.

But if you now expect to hear me say that this led to a great blow-up in my family I have to disappoint you. When I think back on it today nothing much actually happened. Somehow there was nothing there to destroy. Of course we had a big confrontation. I asked my father a question all children ought to ask their parents: "What did you do during the war?" But before my father could answer, my mother intervened, angry, almost screaming, that I should leave my father in peace, he had gone through enough during the war and was glad not to have to talk about it anymore. And when I persisted, saying that in school we had learned about the camps, about the gassing of Jews and the shooting of women and children, and asked whether my father had had anything to do with it, whether he'd been there and participated in those insane deeds, both of them screamed at me. They stood in front of me with angry eyes, one screaming louder than the other, and spoke of their own daughter slandering her parents, of schools that incited children against their own mothers and fathers. Was that the thanks for all their sacrifices and pain, the terrible times they had gone through, the care they had given me? And on and on in that vein. But I didn't let up. I asked the crucial question, whether it was true that Father had worked as a guard in a death camp. At that both of them broke down, cried and whined, and always the same phrases, "That's what you get . . . one's own daughter . . . after everything we've gone through . . . ," etc., etc.

Neither yes nor no. No "I'll try to explain it to you." No guilt. No sorrow. No responsibility. There they sat, the two of them, as though I had accused them of something so bizarre that the only response they could offer was despair and tears. And still, as terrible as that may sound, that's all there was. I continued to go to school, to sit down to dinner with my parents, to go for walks on Sunday, and to celebrate Christmas, as though the mile-wide chasm between myself and my parents had always existed. Today I see everything as through a haze where only outlines are discernible. I feel my way through it, seeing the other person only vaguely, hardly recognizing him, knowing only a little about him, seeing only the same indistinct contours. And however close I get to that other person, everything remains hazy, barely recognizable.

Our family was a working partnership that functioned. I sometimes try to imagine what I would do in a similar situation today. Let's say my husband were to be arrested tomorrow, and it turns out that a few years ago he had murdered someone. He isn't convicted but I know that he is guilty as charged. What would change? Would I leave him, separate from him? Would he suddenly be different from the person I had known? Perhaps I'm not so different from my mother and father. What do I expect of my husband? That he earn enough money so that my children and I can live fairly decently, that he spend his evenings and weekends with us, that he not abuse us and not drink too much. I don't ask for much.

Perhaps my mother didn't expect anything more either. Perhaps she thought, as she packed his lunch pail in the morning, what really mattered is that he be a faithful husband, a hard-working, respected man who looked after his family. But I can't buy the story that she didn't know what his job was. And I found the proof a few months later in my father's desk. One evening —my parents were out—I began to look through his papers. My father's desk, that was almost like a shrine. I found everything there. IDs, working papers, documents, court papers, depositions of witnesses, everything neatly filed away. I looked at the photos on the various IDs. A young, slender face, stern eyes, narrow lips. My father. He hadn't changed all that much over the years. A stranger who was obligated to take care of me. I also found their wedding picture. My mother next to him. Both smiling. That's how they also always smiled at me. The two of them were so strange to me, so remote.

I stayed at home until I graduated from high school, when I moved out. I went to nursing school mostly because they offered housing. I visited my parents every Sunday afternoon. For years I went every Sunday at the same time. My mother would bake a cake, and there was coffee with whipped cream. We talked about my work and about the assorted ailments of old people. Once in a while I tried to steer the conversation to the war and to my father's role. It was pointless. I might just as well have talked to the kitchen sink. Every word I said was washed away. Age did not change them; they remained smooth and ice cold. Then my grandparents died within two years of one another. My father's father had been a civil servant in Frankfurt. Decent, upright people, I had always been told. He'd never been like a real grandfather to me. We saw him every two months, and year in, year out, he always asked me the same question: "Well, Anna, are you making your parents proud?" My mother's father worked for the railroad. I don't know much about him, either. The two grandmothers were much nicer. But aside from a few friendly exchanges during our rare meetings there wasn't any contact. In the space of two years there suddenly were four funerals. I had never before been faced with the death of relatives and dreaded the idea of the funerals. Now I discovered how little it meant to me. There was no real mourning, despite the black dress and my mother's tears. For the first time I asked myself whether I, too, was incapable of mourning, whether the death of another person, even of a relative, meant nothing to me. I tried to imagine what would happen if my parents were run over by a car. Nothing would happen. All it meant was that I would no longer have to visit them for our Sunday coffee.

But please don't misunderstand me. I feel neither particular contempt nor indignation toward them. My main emotion is indifference. The family gradually died. First the grandparents, who certainly must have known everything and never said a word to me. Two years ago my father died. He was sick for a long time. He spent a year in the hospital, and toward the end even in my section. I saw him almost daily. But he remained silent till the very end; not a word about his past crossed his lips. He'd repeat the same old litany whenever I tried to find out anything more. For a while I thought it might be easier, because Mother wasn't there. But it was hopeless. True, he did become a little less rigid and often said how senseless the war had been, that it had robbed him of his youth, and that I'm much better off because now there is no war. He hadn't been a fanatical Nazi but only a man who'd made use of the opportunity to better himself, to make more money. For the rest, everything was duty. Sometimes when he was feverish he'd speak of comrades, as he called them, who'd behaved like swine. But I got nowhere with my questions about what they'd done and where they'd done it. All I got were evasive answers.

My mother and I were with him when he died. For the first time the word "perished" entered my mind. Yes, he perished. I was used to seeing patients die. It happened every day. But some patients perish, die miserably, the way they'd lived. That's how my father died. My mother sat next to his bed and cried. I didn't try to comfort her and I didn't feel pity for my father.

At the time I was already involved with my future husband. He was studying economics. His father was a banking executive. His parents aren't very different from mine, only their way of speaking is a little more refined without saying anything. Paul, my husband, also moved away from home after he finished high school. His father was a judge during the war. Who knows what filthy things he'd done. We married when we were twenty-eight and took an apartment. We invited neither his parents nor mine to our wedding. That was the worst thing we could do to them. For days my mother cried, and his father threatened to disinherit him. But we didn't want them around. We wanted to make a fresh start. No witnesses from the past. Since then we've also begun to pay regular visits to his parents like the ones to my mother. We take turns; one month we visit the one, and one month the other. The two sets of parents have no contact with each other, yet they'd make a good match.

But as I get older I often begin to wonder whether we, my husband and I, are really so very different. And always there's that nagging question about how we would have acted at the time. Let's say my husband comes home tonight and tells me he has the chance of doubling his salary, perhaps even becoming a department head, but for a while he'd have to work in the administrative office of a prison camp. The people there are nothing but dirt anyway, and in taking that job he'd be doing something worthwhile. Would I have reservations? Or would I say that he has to do what he thinks best? Would I ask him what he was really doing there or would I behave as though none of it was my business? These thoughts keep cropping up. Can wolves turn into sheep in the space of a single generation? After all, we are the products of the same parents, the same grandparents, the same teachers, the same priests.

Today I live only for my family. I love my daughters. One is eight, the other ten. They are the first human beings I truly love.

2

Stefanie

The Proud One

MY OLD MAN is as pious as a monk. Everything is kindness and love. But love like in the mind, you know? The first time I stayed out all night he cried and prayed. His idea of love is kissing the other guy's ass. Always walking with your head bent, eyes downcast looking at the shoes. Some father! At times he can be as sweet as a baby. I've never heard him yell. He's either quiet or he cries and prays. You'll never catch him being rough or losing his temper. But his whining is enough to drive a person crazy.

And Mother? She's not all that different. Both of them are Jehovah's Witnesses, waiting for a savior, and when that day comes only they and their friends will be left. The rest of us will go under. A day in our house goes something like this: getting

up—praying—lamenting—praying—crying—praying—going
to bed. Exciting, no?

Well, you know why. They executed my father's old man.
Right after the war. Sometimes, when my mother goes completely crazy, she tells me that I'm possessed by the same devil as
my grandfather. And God will punish me also. That's something
to look forward to. But I won't let them drive me crazy. We're
not allowed to even mention Grandfather, only in our prayers.
They ask God to take pity on him, and they promise to atone for
him through their lives. The only question is, how? They're
ruining themselves, and me along with them, only because the
old man was some kind of big shot under the Nazis. I know him
from pictures. He really looked great. The black uniform, the
boots, what a guy! And that haircut, those eyes. I bet they
were all afraid of him. Not like my old man, who's afraid of
everything.

Say what you will about the Nazis, but they looked great. At
least the men. You can forget about the women with their
blouses and hairdos. But it must have been exciting then. In
school they showed us pictures of parades and rallies. What
enthusiasm! Tell me where you find something like that today.
Yes, I know, it was a bad time. The war, nothing to eat, the
bombs, the Jews. We once had a history teacher. Long hair,
beard, ski sweater, jeans—the works. Boy, did he carry on about
everything. For hours he'd talk about the Jews, the Communists, the Gypsies, the Russians—victims, nothing but victims.
He acted as if he'd been persecuted, as if the Nazis were still
after him. But what was he? He wasn't a Jew or a Gypsy or a
Russian. Maybe a Communist. I never believed the things he
told us. Who knows whether it really was so bad.

Once someone asked him in class: "Tell us, where was the

The Proud One

madness? Why did all those people shout hurrah and Heil? Why was everybody so enthusiastic? There must have been something to it." He just looked stupid, our dear teacher. He called the boy who'd asked the question a neo-Nazi, asked him whether he had no respect for the victims, and so on. But we didn't let up. At least someone finally said it out loud. We wanted to know what things had really been like. It was like a dam had burst. Always that business about criminals and crimes, always us, the Germans. The whole class was yelling and screaming. It was all idiocy, the things he was telling us, one of us said. We'd seen the pictures. The laughing kids, the glowing faces of the women, the streets filled with cheering masses. Where did all that enthusiasm come from? "You're lying," I said to him. At first he looked dumb, but then he let loose. He screamed at us. Gone was that left-wing softy of the sixties. All hell broke loose. At last we had broken through the façade of this all-understanding, all-knowing, all-explaining puppet. Suddenly no more psychobabble. No more words about being able to understand and even accept my aggressions and all that shit. He now went after me in a rage. What could one expect of me, with a grandfather like mine who'd been executed, a criminal, even worse, a war criminal? Those were his exact words. I didn't say a word. But sitting next to me was my friend Gudrun. She suddenly yelled out that he ought to be glad that my grandfather was no longer alive, because . . . That's as far as she got. There was such an uproar that nobody could be heard.

After that our dear teacher really went to pieces. That coward went to the principal. That left-wing hero, always talking about resistance against the powerful, he went to the principal. I can tell you, I know that lying type. The principal then came to our classroom and delivered a long speech. We were covered with guilt and shame, he told us. Maybe he, not I. I didn't murder anyone, I didn't mistreat anyone, I didn't cheer Hitler. If they believe they'd made mistakes, okay. Let them put on a crown of thorns and cry and cry. I'm sick and tired of it. Enough that we Germans are always the bad ones, that we have constantly to be reminded of it. What does that mean—*we* started the war, *we* gassed the Jews, *we* devastated Russia. It sure as hell wasn't me. And no one in my class and none of my friends and certainly not my father. He trembles when he hears a door slam. They executed all the guilty ones back then at Nuremberg. They had their show. My own grandfather was among them. What do they want from me? Every year the same business in school. Movies about concentration camps, pictures of concentration camps, I'm telling you I can't stand it anymore.

Grandma always used to say that Grandfather was murdered. As far as she's concerned there was no guilty verdict and no execution. She's eighty-five now, sits in a wheelchair and talks to herself. She talks about Grandfather only when my father isn't there.

"He was a handsome man," she tells me, "tall, proud, and when he wore his uniform no woman could resist him." Then her face shines. Sometimes she also talks about Hitler. She'd met him a few times. When he walked into a room, she says, they all jumped to their feet and they all were afraid of him, even Grandfather. Unfortunately he went mad at the end, otherwise the war wouldn't have been lost. Well, it all sounds a little crazy, but that's what she tells me. And the Jews, she says, had to be wiped out, to keep them from ruining Germany.

All right, I can imagine what you're thinking. Maybe the old lady is off her rocker, but she's not entirely wrong. Look at the

The Proud One

Jews today. They say none survived. But today they're again all over the place. Do I know any personally? Well, not really. But on TV, the radio, the banks, the newspapers, the Jews are everywhere. An example? Let me think. Well, there's Rosenthal and his "Dalli, Dalli."* Another one? At the moment I can't think of any. I have to ask Grandma, she knows all of them. She always points them out to me: that one's a Jew, and he's a Jew, and so is that one. When she could still get around, she and I would go for walks in our neighborhood. She'd point out the stores that had belonged to Jews. They really controlled almost everything. Now she always says that the little ones were driven out, but the big fish returned. And now they're even richer than before.

Don't misunderstand me. I'm not a racist. I've got nothing against Jews. They don't mean anything to me. I don't even know any. But to keep on accusing me that I with my nineteen years share in the guilt of all the crimes against the Jews, that's ridiculous. What does it mean, we took everything away from them back then? What have we got today? My father was twelve when they took his father away and executed him. His mother was left alone with the children and little money and no honor. For years the old man sacrificed himself "living and fighting for the fatherland," and the reward is a rope around his neck. My father may be a little nuts, but I can't blame him. I can understand why he turned to religion.

You know, sometimes I wouldn't mind being one of those poor little Jews. At least today, not back then of course. But now? Everybody would feel sorry for me, always the big victim.

* Hans Rosenthal, a popular West German game show host, urges contestants on his show to "Dalli, Dalli" ("Hurry up").

They'd shove the money up my behind because of all that bad conscience, and all doors would be open to me. Restitution? That really gets me! Who helped us? Four of us lived in a miserable apartment, in three rooms. Meat once a week. And there was no spending money for the movies or any other fun. What they gave to them they took from me.

Yes, I have a sister. I don't like to talk about her. We don't get along very well. She's three years older than I, and the exact opposite in every respect. Always doing good. Always that gentle manner, enough to make you sick. She's studying medicine and plans to become a psychiatrist. "I live in order to help" is her constant refrain.

Once she almost came to blows with Grandma. They're always at each other's throat. Brigitte, that's my sister, is always on my Grandma. How was it possible for Grandpa to have participated in those crimes? Didn't she have any influence on him? That poor old woman doesn't know what to do. She becomes red in the face and gets very excited. Really furious. "He wasn't a criminal," she says. "He was a hero!" She was and is proud of him, and even though they killed him she will always love him. Then Brigitte gets crazy. They always follow the same script, like roles in a play. And Brigitte also always acts as if it had all happened to her, as if she'd been there.

You can't imagine all the things she's done to rid herself of that great guilt. Atonement, reconciliation—ridiculous. For what? What business is it of hers? I don't understand what she wants. She's just one big crybaby, that's all. Every year she goes to Israel to work in a camp without payment. She's a member of the Committee for Peace, the Committee for International Understanding, the Committee Against Xenophobia, the Committee for Judeo-Christian Amity. She really gets on my nerves, I can tell you. One of these days she'll even form a Committee for Asslickers and appoint herself president.

You ask why I'm so mad at her? It's people like her who destroyed us. The big sister as my model. Don't make me laugh. What should I learn from her? If someone spits at her she offers him a drink because she thinks his mouth is dry. She'll let someone throw a glass of beer in her face and pretend it's raining. She and her friends have no pride. They're worse than the Salvation Army. Are these the new Germans? The future elite, college-trained, our future political leadership? I don't call that humaneness, I call it bad conscience, crawling and afraid. Of course I'm not in favor of a repetition of everything that happened back then. But in that case we need really strong types to prevent it from happening. But my sister and her friends? If they should ever gain control here I'll emigrate.

Where would I go? It doesn't matter, only out of here. Away from these whiners. Given a choice I'd go to a country that hasn't lost a war, or at least not in the last fifty years. For once I'd like to live among victors, not among eternal losers. Look at the French, how proud they are of their country. Or the English, or even the Russians. Would it occur to any of them to hide their nationality when they're in a foreign country? My sister speaks only English when she visits another country so that she won't be taken for a German. Imagine!

You have no such problem, you're an Austrian. First you sent us Hitler and then you were invaded by him. You really arranged it very well, I must say. Today we're the bad ones and you're the victims.

By the way, my mother comes from Austria. From Salzburg. Her parents are still alive. They're very pious. My mother was the one who got my father into Jehovah's Witnesses, to save his soul. But I was left by the wayside because of all that soul-saving.

By the way, I just remembered, I did know one. He was an American soldier. I met him in a disco, and afterward we went to a friend's place. He was wearing a star on a chain around his neck. What do you call it? Star of David, I think. I asked him what it was, and he said that he was a Jew and did I mind? Of course I didn't. Well, that's all there was to it. He wasn't any different than any of the other Americans. Maybe the German Jews are different, I don't know. How can I tell? Nowadays so many dark types are running around here: straight noses, crooked noses, Turks, Italians, Yugoslavs. How's one to tell who's a Jew and who isn't?

How do I think one can tell? You mean by looks? Well, that's a dumb question. Like from pictures or from TV. They probably wouldn't look like my grandpa.

What am I doing now? Nothing. I'm alive. Isn't that enough? I was kicked out of school a year before graduation. It didn't really matter because I never was there anyway. I was already going with Peter. The first thing I did after they kicked me out was to leave home and move in with him. I can tell you, it was crazy. In Peter's dark room I felt I had more space than at home. Then we got married. Real old-fashioned. Peter bought a used Mercedes sports car and we went to Italy. We had a ball, driving around in a convertible. But that, too, had to end. Back in Berlin I tried to find a job. Nothing. The garbage they offer me at the labor office. They're nuts. Am I a Turk or what? I'm bored by it all. They don't find me a job because I didn't graduate. And in school the teachers get on my nerves. It's more than anyone can stand. Well, now I'm sitting around waiting for Peter to come home. He opened his own shop with a friend. No boss. He has

The Proud One

the right idea. Maybe I'll go and work with him if I don't find anything else.

Do you think that back then they were as frustrated as they try to tell us? I'd like to feel as proud as they did then. Head high and belief in the future. Even if things fell apart, but until they did it must have been quite something. I'd like to feel that good. And let me tell you, I will. At any rate I won't be like my father. What became of this old officer family? In Grandma's photo album all the men are in uniform. Not only Grandpa, but his father and his father's father also. All of them looking great. We were somebody. General so-and-so and spouse, Field Marshal so-and-so and spouse, and so on. Grandma and Grandpa lived in a villa in the Grunewald,* not like us, in three rooms in Moabit.† They had a chauffeur and six servants, Grandma says. And there was excitement. Tea with a minister and his wife, Baron so-and-so for dinner, balls, receptions. I don't know if everything Grandma tells me is true, but it sure sounds great. Maybe the old man, as they were stringing him up, thought that it was all worthwhile. What had he done that was so terrible that they hanged him? Nobody has been able to explain that to me. Over and over again I've asked my old man that question. And always the same answer: "He was an evil man." And that he was possessed by the Devil, has millions on his conscience, brought disaster on mankind, and so forth. Not a single simple explanation, at least not any that I can understand. Who was he? A sorcerer? A circus magician who could make people disappear? I don't know. Maybe I'm too stupid to understand any of it, or maybe it's the fault of the people who are telling it to me.

* An upper-middle-class section of Berlin.
† A working-class district of Berlin.

But most of the time I got no answer at all. As soon as the topic turned to Grandpa, my old man and old lady immediately began to pray. But let me tell you, nobody can convince me that it's shameful to be German. That time is over. Peter and our friends agree with me. Those bleeding hearts of the sixties can go to hell. Let them move to the country, plant vegetables, eat mush, and raise free-ranging chickens. I don't like the Greens. They don't have any of the new pride. They're afraid of atomic war, of chemical industries, of dying forests, of the census. Every day they tell us that all of us will soon die. Stand around in Parliament in their jeans and preach the end of the world. They're like my parents.

Do I have any particular ideal? How do you mean that?

Can you name anyone here in Germany that I can admire? Who are our models? Yesterday's old Nazis? Or the new Greens? Or people like my parents who are wasting their lives in fear? Who do you think are the models for people in my age group? There's nothing. Nobody.

We're the last of the Mohicans.

Who do I think is great? I'm great!

3

Rudolf

The Guilty One

FIRST OF ALL I must tell you that I'm haunted by guilt. And people who are guilty are punished, if not here and now then in another place. My turn is sure to come. There's no escape. But you'll learn nothing from me. Not a word. What they did will remain a secret. No one will find out. Their deeds, or rather, their misdeeds, shall not be mentioned anywhere. Not a single word, except the guilt now rests on my shoulders. My parents, they're already roasting in hell. They died a long time ago; it's over for them, this life. But they left me behind. Born in guilt, left behind in guilt.

The dreams are worst of all. Always at night they come and get me. Always the same dream. I know it like a movie I've seen a hundred times. They tear me from my bed, drag me through the room, down the stairs, and push me into a car. They're men wearing striped uniforms. The car races through a city. There's noise all around. People shout "Hurrah," yelling and screaming. Sometimes I think we're driving through a street in which the people cheer us. We arrive at a house I don't recognize. I'm pushed down the stairs into a cellar, they rip my pajamas off and push me into a room. The door closes behind me. Do I have to tell you what room it is?

There are showerheads on the wall, and through the openings something streams out with a soft hiss, like air from a defective bicycle tire. I have trouble breathing; I think I'm choking. I rush to the door, try to open it, rattle it, scream, my eyes are burning. Then I wake up. Usually I then get up and don't go back to bed. I can't sleep anymore. As soon as I close my eyes it starts all over again. They tear me out of bed, and so on.

There was a time when I had this dream twice a week. Then again I didn't have it for months, and then it would start all over again.

Doctors? I've been to dozens. The ones I liked best were the ones who asked me what I thought the dream meant, why I think I have the dream. Are they crazy or am I? Should I tell them that I . . . Shit!

Sometimes I imagine that I'm murdering someone. I choose somebody I don't know at random, murder him, and then turn myself in to the police. Everything would then be over. I'd spend the rest of my life in prison, where I belong, to make up for my father, who didn't go there. They would torture me, beat me, and all day long I'd have to do some idiotic work. But all that is preferable to what I have now. Just look at me. Innocent, I am living the life of a guilty person.

My parents escaped to South America. New name, new passport, a new beginning in the "free world." But not anonymously, oh no. Among lots of friends and fellow soldiers. We moved from city to city, and everywhere we were expected, called for by car, friends welcomed us, a new house—everything was there, and a new life began. Until we left once more and were received someplace else. We were expected wherever we went. I was born in 1950. By the time I was ten we had moved four times. After that things calmed down. We stayed in a South American country; apparently they'd stopped looking for us. Or at least they didn't find us. You won't believe it, but later we got our German passports back.

Today I am a German, a German bearing the identity of the son of a criminal. A life sentence. Reason: son of a murderer. Sentenced to parents who'd led the lives of butchers. How do I know what they'd really done?

Perhaps my dear father sent the women that he took from the camp at night into the gas chambers the next morning. Or perhaps he kept them and helped them. And maybe my darling mother sent her driver back to hard labor because he didn't polish the car just so. And then she got herself a new driver.

He hadn't done anything. She hadn't done anything. After all, what's all the excitement about? Driving the truck into a Polish village, rounding up Jews, taking them to the cemetery, the men here, the women there. The men dig a long trench while the women and children strip and neatly pile up their clothing and jewelry. Once, one single time, my father was drunk enough to talk about it, how terrible it had been, that time they had to shoot the children one by one with a handgun because those idiotic soldiers had aimed their automatic weapons too high above the heads of the adults.

Oh my God, my dear papa. What a good man! He cried when he talked about it. What bad times those were, he whined.

Thank God it's over. But there he was wrong, my dear papa. It'll never be over. Do you know the song "They're Coming To Take Me Away"?

I keep on humming it to myself. Let me tell you, one day they'll come. They've already gotten my parents. They were killed in a car accident in 1968. In a second it was all over. They were burned to death beyond recognition. It was gorgeous, like an atomic blast. Unfortunately I didn't see it, but I would have liked to. Both of them were buried in Argentina, even though my father in his will said he would like to be buried in Germany. I didn't do it. I prevented it. None of his wishes were to be granted once he was dead. No more orders, no more edicts.

The night after the funeral I went back to the cemetery and pissed on his grave. I trampled on it, went crazy, cried. It was terrible. That was my farewell. I never went back there. And when I die I don't want to be buried there.

Why did they get that insane notion, after everything that had happened, to make a child? To pretend to be a family. To live like devils and die like angels, how is that possible? We were always well off, we had everything. There was always enough money. "Project Reinhard," does that mean anything to you? In our neighborhood there were a lot of Germans, many with a past like my parents'. All of them were doing well. Big houses, swimming pools, servants. The money came from "Reinhard." All of them had taken their little packets with them from Germany.

When I was ten my old man opened a real estate business. He brought all his old comrades into the neighborhood. Many of them were already there. Everything around us was German: German schools, German stores, church on Sunday, followed by beer at the tavern. German friends, German jokes, and German papers. Yes, of course, also Austrians. But for the rest we were among our own. German victors. Not a trace of defeat. We knew the bombed-out houses only from pictures. Here things were always in bloom. Eternal spring, fertile soil, a victor's paradise. Why was I born? Does this question mean anything to you? It was asked by Jodl* after he was sentenced to death. Quite a question, no?

I've read everything that was said at that trial. Frank† was the only one who voiced any regrets. I have often tried to imagine what my father would have said. I don't think he would have voiced a single word of regret, not a single word about his guilt. When he was sober he was a hero. A victor. His voice was always a little louder than that of others, always serious, decisive. He never just smiled; he laughed outright, loud, and then immediately again became serious and businesslike. Above all, just and consistent. If the cook was ten minutes late he'd fire her. He checked the lawn after it was cut. When a new maid was hired she was told how to line up the glasses in the wall cabinet.

Punishment was administered ritually. I had to stand against the wall with raised arms. Then he would hit me across the rear end five times with a thin bamboo stick. My mother would stand next to him and watch, after which she'd take me into her arms and console me. Father would leave the room. Afterward I had to go to his room and apologize. After all, I had hurt the poor man's feelings.

Once some money was missing from a bowl on my father's desk. Not much. He used to keep small change there for tips. He decided to show us how such matters are handled. After dinner

* General Alfred Jodl, executed at Nuremberg.
† Hans Frank, the Nazi administrator of Poland, executed at Nuremberg.

he called the servants in. The cook, the maid, the gardener. Striding back and forth, he told them they had an hour to report the culprit or they'd all be fired.

I was twelve at the time. It was an important day in my life. I screamed at my father to leave them alone, that I was the one who had taken the money. Enraged, my father sent the servants away, all the while yelling like crazy. Do you know why? Because I had said it in Spanish, had humiliated him in front of the servants. My first puny triumph over him. I was proud. I'd made the great hero lose his temper.

Not far from us lived a group of Jewish emigrants, all Germans. Half of the kids in some of our classes were Jews and the other half non-Jews, mostly the children of old Nazis.

But outside of school there was no contact. On the contrary, there were frequent fights, real gang activity. I was never a fighter. I was a pudgy child, ate lots of sweets, and was always the loser in fights. A real officer's son. But the others had formed a gang and played war games. They'd attack one of the Jews and beat him up, and then the Jews would get one of ours, and so it went, back and forth. I was never really part of this; they didn't want me, and anyway, they got on my nerves.

And so I had no friends, neither among the ones nor the others. I kept to myself. Like a stillbirth being kept alive artificially. An artificial kidney, an iron lung, and a plastic heart, assembled and supplied with arms and legs.

The last three years before their deaths I made my parents' lives hell. I was eighteen when they died. When I was fifteen I began to hang out with other men and boys. When my parents realized that I was gay they wanted to kill me, or maybe first me and then themselves. Perhaps their car accident wasn't really an accident.

"Back home they would have pinned a pink triangle on you," my mother shouted at me. She had to know. But those days were gone. There in Argentina, with my blond hair and blue eyes, I was a hit. I could have anyone I wanted.

So, as you can see, their planned rebirth didn't work. The new beginning of my dear parents in South America turned into a dead end. And at first it had all seemed so promising. A new beginning in a country without a war. The success, the lovely house, the friends, the Christmas tree, the children's choir, Hitler's birthday, all the feast days and holidays. They weren't afraid. Not after 1960. It was all forgotten. Life was back to pre-1945 Germany, that is, until my mother found gay pornography under my bed, until they got something from me that they'd never suspected. I caught them unawares and they collapsed. These upright, indestructible people collapsed and disintegrated.

It was all over for German honor. Once they realized that I was gay they drew back. They never discussed it with me. As a matter of fact, there was very little conversation of any kind. No more visitors, no beer in the tavern, no honorary positions on the carnival committee. They crawled into their shells like snails. They were ashamed of me, the poor souls. For the first time in their lives they were ashamed.

Once I realized how vulnerable I made them I became completely uninhibited. I brought my friends home, dressed like a fag, and in front of visitors talked like a fag. I really let them have it.

You should have been there. Within months my parents

changed completely. Then I was kicked out of school for sexual molestation. My father was called to the principal. I hope it was the worst day of his life.

I am convinced that anything, even being charged with murder, would have been preferable. But his son a fag?

I must not have any children. This line must come to an end with me. What should I tell the little ones about Grandpa? I lived with my parents too long, who knows what evil I carry within me? It mustn't be handed down. It's over, our proud noble lineage. If anyone should ask, the "von" [from] in my name at most means "from where." But soon there'll be nobody to ask.

The last few years before my parents' death I just hung around. I'd been kicked out of school, didn't look for work, and my parents no longer bothered about me. I read a lot, especially about the Third Reich, everything I could lay my hands on. And over and over again I came across my father's name. I don't want to mention it here; it must remain a deeply buried secret. But I can assure you that anyone who knew my parents knows exactly who is meant. Won't they be shocked! I can't wait to see their faces.

I soon found out who my father was, yet it was as though I had always known it anyway. Actually I learned nothing new. All I got was a confirmation of my assumptions and suspicions. A picture began to take shape in my mind, a combination of the things I had read and the things my father had talked about. And also my mother's occasional offhand remarks. Everything suddenly fell into place. Maybe I killed them. Maybe they drove into that tree on purpose. But why wasn't I in the car with them?

The Guilty One

After my parents' death I sold everything and came to Germany. After all, I had a German passport. And all the money I needed.

The last few years I haven't done a damn thing. I don't have to work, at least not as long as the money lasts. I can't go to college because I didn't finish high school, and I don't feel like taking makeup exams. I haven't done a thing for fifteen years. I am a professional failure. I was programmed to fail.

At times I wish it were all over. Hanging around and waiting makes no sense. I hope they come to get me soon.

4

Johannes

The Innocent One

I DON'T THINK yours is the right approach. Today it's no longer a question of whether the past has been overcome or whether it lives on in someone like me. What matters now is whether you, I, and all of us together are willing to get rid of the hatred that lives in all of us and replace it with love, understanding, and oneness. Communality, coming together, mutual understanding is our only hope. But for that to happen we must put the past behind us once and for all, bury it. Together. Let us jointly turn toward new goals. Peace, justice, equality of the sexes, the foreign-worker situation, unemployment, disarmament—there are enough insoluble problems to keep us busy for a long time. Why go on living in the past? After all, there are more important things we Germans must do. Let's visit the past in museums or read about it in history books. We mustn't allow it to rob us of the energy for the here and now, let alone the future, for we will need all our strength to save Germany from new disaster. Still, let us not condemn those who continue to live in the past. We must try to enter into their minds, to feel with them, and above all, to be frank with each other. One day love will conquer all. Love is the only power, the only true power."

How do you like this little tract? I prepared it when I knew you were coming today. That's how I thought I'd talk to you.

But now let's be honest. I'll tell you about myself, candidly and openly. My parents were evil, vile. There was poison in their blood, their breath reeked of sulphur. Yet they didn't have vampire teeth and they didn't have horns. They looked no different than the resistance fighters who were executed. Same looks, same faces, same dress, same haircuts. They weren't marked on the outside, and as far as one could tell, not on the inside either.

My father worked for the railroad. Before the war, during the war, and after the war. A petty bureaucrat of high position, a man who'd started on the bottom and worked his way up to the very top, but who nonetheless remained a petty bureaucrat at heart. Decent, respectable, incorruptible. First he was a member of the Communist party, then of the Nazis, and at the end of the Social Democrats. A steadily rising career without any surprises, without flaws or unexpected hitches. His railroad system transported striking workers during the Weimar Republic, hikers during the thirties, soldiers and concentration camp prisoners in the forties, and when the war was over, hikers again. Anyone who paid the fare was allowed on the trains, regardless of destination. His work was his life. To him job performance was a physical concept—a given amount of work within a given amount of time. Merely doing a job was not enough. He took pride in the way he did his job, in not being a mere machine. Actively doing rather than just functioning, a human switch in a circuit. The amount of work to be done within a given time period was the law by which he lived. Can you imagine what it was like having such a father? It was like looking at a modern nonrepresentational painting. You stand in front of it and think you can make out a form and yet you can't understand what it means. Still you don't give up. You want to understand it. For years I tried to understand my father. I had almost given up, when a chance occurrence brought me insight into him.

I was fourteen at the time. Like every year, we were spending our vacation in Italy. My parents loved Italy. We always went to the same campsite on the Adriatic. The only difference this time was that we were mugged and robbed. A harmless business. A couple of motorcyclists stopped our car as we were coming back from a restaurant. They made us get out of the car, took our money and cameras, and let us go. The whole thing took at most two or three minutes.

And my father? What did he do? He went down on his knees before them and cried in fear. He pleaded and sobbed, begged them not to hurt him, to take anything they wanted, only not hurt him. . . .

I was fascinated by his fear, his disintegration, his cruel cowardice. Boundless fear, that was his dirty little secret. He always had to be on the side of the strong. What else could he do?

His life was an object lesson in survival. He saved every membership card of every organization he'd ever belonged to. When I went through his desk after his death I found them all.

The Innocent One

He was fully paid up in each of them. His was more than a case of simple adjustment. It was a sort of dissolution of the ego, a denial of the self. He always turned into that which seemed to pose a threat.

He never criticized anyone. I never heard him rail against the Nazis or against the left or the right; there were no adversaries, only like-minded people, like-minded superiors. It was a system that functioned because of his transformation into what was expected of him before an order was even given. He had the gift of anticipating the needs of those about to take power and to prepare for them. He did the same thing with me. I can't recall a conversation between us when I didn't feel as though I'd been caught unawares. He knew how to hand on the fear that consumed him. His relentless bad conscience made my life hell. My childhood fantasies centered on how to become a criminal without being caught. I dreamed of robbing a bank, of mugging people without being caught. I was fascinated by the idea of the undetected crime. The eternally hounded, never apprehended perpetrator. To be constantly hunted, almost caught.

At school I began to steal. When I was fifteen I systematically went through the lockers of the other kids and took everything I could put my hands on. Combs, bus passes, pencils, marbles, and, of course, money. I had quite a cache in my desk at home. I set aside two drawers for my loot and divided it into neatly labeled categories. You see, I started early. The way you see me here today, on this special visit, is how I began early on. A seamless career, just like my father's. But right now let's get back to my school days. The things I took I saved, and I spent the money. They never caught me. Everyone of course knew that there was a thief among us. Once the principal even called in the police and they questioned us. They asked us where we were at a given time, when we left school, but they didn't have a chance of catching me. I lied like a trouper. And they believed every word. There was never the slightest suspicion that I might be the culprit. Anyway, nobody would have believed it possible. I was an ordinary child, skinny, nondescript, neatly dressed, modest, and undemanding. But behind that façade there was steel. I personified the fine line between harmless and innocuous. Apparently nothing complicated lay hidden underneath the simple surface. But not so. This guise of naïveté and innocence was the most exciting outer appearance I could devise to hide the simple, petty thief underneath.

At the time this adventure seemed like a triumph. To go unpunished yet not be acquitted. Without expiating, and free of guilt or recriminations, I continued to steal. My technique became more sophisticated; I stole more and more, and my cache grew bigger and bigger. That is, until I got bored. Superiority can also become boring.

When I was eighteen my father retired. Three months later he died. My mother is still alive. She lives quietly by herself on my father's pension. A small, slender, nice lady. She talks to me the same way as to the local shopkeeper, the taxi driver, or the child that happens to sit next to her on the bus. A year after my father's death my mother told me that my father wasn't that nice, decent man I may have thought. She told me about the transports of Jews, journeys to extermination camps. She spoke of participation and joint responsibility, and even of shared guilt. She meant well, but it was too late. What could still be rectified? There had been silence for too long. He was dead, the perpe-

The Innocent One

trator was dead. And there was nothing I could do; I couldn't confront him with it.

My mother meant well. She became nicer, and sometimes even affectionate. Still, the closer she tried to get, the faster I ran away. I found her newly discovered love for me, her son, intolerable. I was disgusted by her belated attempt, now that her husband was dead, to start a new life with me. My father had slipped out of reach, and my mother wasn't enough for me. But my own life? I don't know, it's hard to say. I remember so few details. Everything always went like clockwork. Every day the same routine—school, coming back home, dinner. There was never much conversation. My mother's recurrent phrase was "You know." "You know that Father doesn't like this. You know that Sundays we always eat at seven. You know that we work this hard to make a better life for you."

I knew it all. I knew of their good intentions. Their determined effort for a better future was touching. I believe that my father really meant it, say what you will about him, about his blinders, his coldness, his methodical life. Every day, every move, every action had to be exactly like the one before. That's what made him happy. Still, he wasn't malicious, at least not intentionally. It's not that he wanted evil, but he was afraid to do good if it involved even the slightest resistance to authority. I think he simply didn't recognize the difference between good and evil. I believe it was the writer Erich Kästner who said that there is no such thing as good in the abstract, only doing good. In the case of my father, this would have to read that there is no such thing as good in the abstract, only the failure to do good.

For Christmas I always got homemade toys. Father would spend weeks making something, a car or a wheelbarrow or some other wooden toy. The actual giving of the gifts tended to become extremely strenuous. My parents would stand there, eyes fixed on me, mouths open, waiting for me to open the huge package. Then some lacquered monstrosity would emerge from the paper, and, you won't believe it, I actually loved it. Yes, really, I was thrilled. At least till I was around twelve or thirteen. Other festivities also followed the same routine for years. Easter, for example. It went according to a strict plan. Some colored eggs, chocolate, hidden all over the living room. Both my parents would stand in the doorway and watch me hunt for the gifts, and whenever I found something they smiled. After that everything was put into a basket and I was allowed to have a piece a day. It would never have occurred to me to take a second piece or eat it all up in one day. Only years later, in my adolescence, did I begin to wonder about this senseless repetitive behavior. But what was so special about all this? Nothing, absolutely nothing. I couldn't even tell you that my old man ever said anything nasty about anyone. No racism, no vilification of blacks or Jews or gays.

He was a little shorter than I, with dark hair which he wore combed back, plastered down like a helmet. His shoulders were a bit rounded, and when he walked he seemed in danger of tripping. But he never did. He changed his underwear every other day. Every Monday, Wednesday, and Friday my mother laid out a fresh pair of socks, shorts, undershirt, and shirt for him, and he put on whatever she'd laid out, never changing a thing. Every May he went with Mother to buy a summer suit, and in September a winter suit. I knew every item of clothing he wore. Every movement was predictable. There were no surprises, except for that incident in Italy I mentioned. If it hadn't been for that I'd never have seen that other side of him.

I often tried to imagine how the two slept together. Their bedroom was next to mine. A heavy wardrobe stood against our adjoining wall in my room to cushion any sounds. However, if I opened the wardrobe and put my ear against the wall I could hear what the two of them were doing. And it was as regular as everything else in their lives. They did it every Wednesday. I would count the squeaks of the bedsprings. By the time I got to twenty-five it was all over. No moaning, no groans. Twenty-five times squeak squeak, and then quiet for another week. And he died as he had lived. One day after dinner he lay down for a nap. When my mother tried to wake him an hour later—he favored an hour-long after-dinner nap—she found him dead. No screams, no desperate effort to get out of bed. He just lay there and was dead, leaving this world, this small, nasty world which he handed on to me.

Why didn't I ever punch him in the mouth, even once? But my life went on. After finishing high school I went to work in a bank. I got the job through a friend of my father's, naturally. I liked working with figures, percentages, dividends, checks. A leap from my little world into the big world of finance. A single signature of an officer could move more money than I could make in ten years.

To be honest, even then I was obsessed by just one idea: the best way to dump on these types. What interested me wasn't so much a big bank robbery but rather how to break into the computerized money transactions. I became a workaholic. My superiors were enthusiastic, my mother was impressed, and everybody predicted great things for me. And my career did indeed take off. I continued to move up the ladder, to ever larger desks and more comfortable chairs, to more expensive suits and cars. I was a success. When I became a branch manager I began to embezzle money with the help of a complicated yet simple system. Every month I managed to transfer around 10,000 DM to Switzerland. I don't even remember exactly what I did with all the money. Trips, gambling, occasionally in the company of a lady friend. Every other month I took off for a long weekend. On Friday morning I'd go to Zurich to pick up the money, and from there to Nice or Rome or Monte Carlo. For three days I was in control—a gentleman, a prince. I'd tip a doorman more than I made in a day.

These few days were my new life. Here I became a new person. No one asked where I came from, who my parents were, what I did for a living. Money bought complete anonymity. I didn't renounce my past, but I paid a fortune to be rid of it for a few days. I paid with everything I had—with money and with my freedom. But it was worth it. Do you know what it means to live without a past? I extinguished my past. I paid the people I came in contact with to ignore me, to refrain from investigating where and whom I came from. I never had the feeling of wronging anyone. The law? Justice? What ridiculous notions. All I had to do was take what I needed. My disguise was of course expensive, but it was essential to me. Naturally I was caught. I confessed and I got eight years. I've already done three, and in view of my good behavior I'll probably be let out sooner. I'm already allowed out every other Sunday.

The question is what does all this have to do with my father's life. He never broke any laws. On the contrary, he was the personification of probity. Whoever his superior, whatever the system, he was a model citizen. It was my mother who a year

The Innocent One

after his death tried to tell me that he was rotten, that he'd been the helper of butchers and murderers, a man who would hand the rope to the executioner after checking its strength. Chief of the materiel section, responsible for technical problems, not for human beings. Today I have the luxury of deciding whom I despise more, my father or my mother. How lovely it would be, a life without a past. Sometimes I wish that both of them had died while I was still small.

5

Rainer and Brigitte

The Separables

RAINER: I'm Rainer, and this is Brigitte, my sister. We're the children of a Nazi family. Our father was—

BRIGITTE: We're not the children of a Nazi family, but of a military family. I know that we don't agree about our parents, but maybe we can agree on terminology.

RAINER: Have it your way. I really don't care. You can stick to your version. As far as I'm concerned, ours was a family of Nazis, or perhaps better still, a family of war criminals. Not every Nazi was a war criminal, but our father managed to be both.

BRIGITTE: I won't cooperate if that's how you're going to start. I don't feel like being put on the defensive by you from the word go. In that case let's forget about the interview altogether. Anyway, I think it's stupid to air our differences about our father

The Separables

before the whole world. Either we skip the personal interpretation or I leave.

RAINER: All right, let's be completely objective. Our father —how should I put it—was a high-ranking officer in the German army. He and his fellow officers on the General Staff planned whatever measures were needed to do away with the subhumans. He created living space for Germans, brought back wheat from the Ukraine, oil from Rumania, and coal from Poland. For him war was a game played with colored pins on a map. A few divisions to the north here, a few to the south there, planes on the right, tanks on the left. And victory was tantamount to pulling off a successful business deal.

BRIGITTE: Your cynicism won't do you any good. He was your father! I can still see you sitting on his lap while he read to you or played soccer with you in the garden or took your hand on walks when you got tired. He was your father, your ideal and your hero. You didn't know anything about his past, and you wouldn't have cared. You were born after the war, you didn't witness the final months of the collapse. What do you know about bombing raids, about fleeing from the Russians, about our panic when Father was arrested? And then came his prison sentence. Our neighbors, all those good friends—suddenly they all turned into dyed-in-the-wool anti-Nazis. Mr. M., that swine, still lives in his "Aryanized" villa nearby. But at the trial he testified against Father. Our father spent four years in prison. Can you tell me why? Millions went off to war with enthusiasm, thousands participated in the persecution of the Jews and profited from it. Our father behaved decently throughout. He never took a single item of confiscated Jewish property. He paid for his house out of his own pocket. He never had anything to do with the SS, nor with concentration camps or the execution of women and children. He was a soldier, not a criminal. I don't understand how you can talk about him like this.

RAINER: He wasn't simply one or the other, either my father *or* a criminal. He was both. And that's what I hold against him. How could he play ball with me as though nothing had happened? What other games was he playing simultaneously in his lifetime? General, father, husband, and finally bank executive, his last, respectable position. I can remember when I was little, Mother always ordered me not to bother him, not to disturb him. Later, when I went to school, she asked me not to tell him when I got poor marks, for that too would only upset him. And still later, when I took part in student demonstrations, I was again warned not to upset him. I always had to spare him, not bother him with my problems, my concerns, but only bring him joy—a playful, happy youngster. Was he ever a real father to me? He was like a household pet entrusted to our care. All that caution and consideration, that don't-come-too-close-to-the-poor-man business. That's the way we sidestepped all conflicts, all frank discussions. One word about the Nazis and Mother would stare icily and launch into her litany: "Leave Father alone! He's gone through enough! Seven years of war and four years of prison is more than enough for one lifetime." And he'd just sit there listening like a stuffed doll.

BRIGITTE: That's not how I remember your childhood. I remember you as a six-year-old, coming home proudly with your first report card and your swimming medals, or the two of you going off to the movies on a Sunday afternoon, or you asking Father to read to you. Do you think a little child can be lied to? He loved you and was a good father to both of us, you as well as me. I think your hateful tirades are really directed more against yourself than against him. The things you've done to turn yourself into a victim! You're terrified because you're the son of someone who committed a crime, and that fear has done terrible things to you. Don't kid yourself, you are and will always be the son of a German officer, and neither your stay in a kibbutz in Israel nor your disquisitions about fascism at the university can change that. You'll always be the son of a German officer, even if you get involved in street brawls with alleged Nazis. I remember that there was a time when you even toyed with the idea of converting to Judaism. What's all that supposed to mean? Do you think that this sort of thing will help you throw off your past? Can't you understand? You're the offspring of German officers, and that's in your blood, just as it is in mine. And even if you were to become a rabbi it wouldn't change a thing.

RAINER: You talk as though you'd never been troubled by any of this.

BRIGITTE: I wasn't because I was proud of our father. He had the courage to join a movement that held out the promise for a better future. I always defended him because I understood him; I defended him in school against the lying teachers who overnight had turned into antifascists, against so-called friends who thought it would be exciting to go to bed with the daughter of a well-known Nazi, and against all those others who wanted to bring back the past and thought I was their ally. I know what happened back then. You don't have to act the schoolmaster with me. But I also know that when my father joined the Nazis in the thirties he did so enthusiastically, convinced that what he was doing was right. But reproaching him or me won't turn you into something you aren't.

RAINER: Stop it! It makes me sick to hear you talk in these generalities. What do you mean that he believed he was doing the right thing, that he acted out of conviction? Couldn't he see back in 1933 what they were after? Couldn't he have pulled back after the Kristallnacht? Couldn't he at least have joined the 20th of July group? Do you want to know what our father was? A coward! A criminal coward! A milksop! A puppet with pension rights! His enemies weren't the Russians or French or British. His enemies were the Germans, the Germans in his own country. And that's why he hated me so toward the end of his life, because I was like those Germans he thought he had exterminated with the help of his party. He hated me because I was able to say no. He hated me because I wasn't as scared as he. He always believed that the war and the party would create a new type of German, or at the least that Germans would be the only survivors. But he was the old type of German. And I hope this old type will soon become extinct.

BRIGITTE: You're just as scared as he, only you're scared of different things. You don't know how much alike you are. That same fanaticism, only now in the opposite camp. Your implacable righteousness is inhuman. Just listen to yourself when you talk about political enemies. I've often thought that back then Father must have sounded just like that. Perhaps it's sheer accident that you're on the opposite side. I think I'm very different. I try to understand people, why they act the way they do and why they are what they are. But you want to live in an either/or world, a world of either friends or enemies. That's how it was back then. Tell me, what is the difference between you and your father?

RAINER: My fanaticism, not your impotence or so-called understanding, will prevent the resurgence of fascism. Yes, I'm waging war on the German past. I long for the day when the last survivor of the Third Reich will be dead. I look forward to their

The Separables

extinction. Perhaps then we'll finally get a chance for a new Germany.

BRIGITTE: You're dreaming. Nothing will change. If you were in power today you'd hang the others. Your concentration camps would be just as full as those old ones. You and your friends can't fool me. For two hundred years the men in our family were officers. But until you came along they at least were real men. Even after he came out of prison Father held his head high, and emaciated though he was he carried himself with pride. You're not the new, wonderful breed you think you are. Your left-wing enthusiasm was nothing but spite against Father. Just think of how you decorated your room. Ridiculous! A Mao portrait here, a Lenin picture there, a Marx bust on the desk. Later that Star of David on a neck chain, and after that a Palestinian shawl draped over your shoulders. What other disguises do you still need? Do you want me to go on? Just look at yourself!

RAINER: I've always tried my best to become a new type of German, not to be like my father. What's wrong with that? But he wouldn't help me. He harped on the neutrality of soldiers. All he cared about was obligation and duty. He gave his allegiance to whatever government was in power. But what about the duty to disobedience? That meant nothing to him. Only once, toward the end of his life, did he talk more frankly about those times. He told me that his fellow officers said among themselves that the war had to be won before Hitler could be overthrown, that they had every intention to try and build a democratic society after the war. After the war! What a mixture of naïveté and madness! He really thought that the war could be won. I still can't believe it.

BRIGITTE: You don't know what you're talking about. Or

you do and are distorting the facts. It was the General Staff that warned Hitler against marching into Austria, against occupying the Rhineland and Czechoslovakia, and they even tried to prevent the war against Poland. In 1938 Jodl even said that Hitler had the entire country behind him except for the General Staff. But you acted like a beast, trampling on Father even when he was already old. What kind of heroism do you call it, insulting an old, sick man?

RAINER: Stop kidding yourself. Father was the last link in a chain of generations of order-takers and masochistic obeyers, officer after officer, from Prussian to fascist, following orders. I'm proud to be the one who's breaking this tradition. For two hundred years the men in our family handed on to their offspring a tradition of unconditional obedience. I, thank God, have broken the chain, the first nonmilitarist in maybe a hundred and fifty years. No more moving around divisions on drawing boards, with a few thousand casualties here and another handful there.

What do you think went through his mind? Actually you're right, toward the end he'd turned into a nice old man. I don't understand how he could have done the things he did.

BRIGITTE: Tell me, do you honestly think he was a mass murderer? Or is it all a farce? Did you see him hanging around with concentration camp guards and SS murderers? I can't believe you. Your indignation is so ridiculously hysterical, so forced. You shout and rave, smash things. What is it all supposed to mean? You should have seen yourself, how excited you used to get. And your women! Unbelievable. Sometimes it was almost funny, those last surviving hippies coming out of your room dressed in panties and nothing on top, smoking pot. I was always tempted to ask you whether you were doing this for our

The Separables

benefit, to show Father how unconventional you were? Or did you want to shock us with that glimpse of bosom and behind? Rainer the scourge of the bourgeoisie! Laughable! Why didn't you move out? Why didn't you refuse to take the money? Why didn't you leave the family and start from scratch someplace else? That I could have understood. But your protest was underwritten by Father. Every Mao tract you bought was paid for by the bank where Father worked. And even the grass for your funny cigarettes came from him. You never earned a single penny. I feel sorry for you.

RAINER: Spare me your pity. It's nice to know that you feel sorry for me. But it won't do you any good, nor me, because I still hate him even though he's dead. All those ridiculous things I did were an attempt to defend myself against him. At least I tried, unlike you. Your whole life was an exercise in accommodation, a desperate effort not only to please him but to follow in his footsteps. Just look at your husband! A poor replica of Father. He, too, works in the bank, and who knows, he might even become its president if he continues to kiss enough important asses. When you sit at the table with Mother and your husband I can see Father sitting next to you. Nothing has changed. You talk like him, act like him, and even read the same books. You can be proud of your life, that senseless rerun of a senseless life. But basically you're right. I've lost my battle. All my ridiculous efforts, as you call them, to become someone else have been in vain. But do you know why I've failed? Because Mother and you—and I hold you primarily responsible, because Mother after all was married to him—didn't help me. I suddenly found that I had to fight not one but the three of you, and for that I was too weak. I've become resigned. I'm too weak to begin again; I live at home like a child and am afraid of being kicked out. My battle is over, my goals are shrouded in mist. I have lost. My future? I don't want any, it doesn't interest me. If Father can't be vanquished then there is no future for me. Because his life is not a life I care to live. Or do you think I should apply at the bank?

BRIGITTE: Stop whining. Again that victimization. You're not a victim of your father. At best, you're the victim of your bizarre demands and objectives. I don't care whether or not you go to the bank. Do whatever you want, but do me one favor— stop crying. Neither of us has it easy, I know that. We more than most others come of a family that lost the war, because ours helped start it. All of us, not only you, lost. And it is not all that simple to pull oneself up out of this nothingness, this abyss. We were vanquished, and like a defeated fighter we drag ourselves to the locker room and try, slowly, to regain our strength. The scars of that fight are visible on and in us. Some healed and some will never heal, and perhaps will even be handed on to our children. But that's our fate, a hard fate for us, the children of those who caused and started it all. But perhaps it's also an opportunity. I don't know. And I don't see it. I really don't want anything more than to be left in peace. Let our children make a better job of it.

RAINER: So you're also resigned, just like me. That almost reassures me. I always thought you were much stronger than I. Strange, but now I feel connected to you, more than ever before. Suddenly I don't seem to care how you feel about Father.

BRIGITTE: I'm sorry to have to disillusion you, but you're just as much of a stranger to me as ever. I don't want to share in your suffering. I manage things differently. I don't crawl and don't turn myself into an innocent bystander by pretending that I, along with thousands of others, am the victim of my father. I don't want that, can't you understand it? I don't want to be someone to be sorry for, and no one except I myself am responsible for my fate. And if my life with my husband is a continuation of my parents' life, it still is my own decision, my own will. And I've never relinquished it, regardless of who my father was and what he was guilty of. I am not the child of a perpetrator. I am not the child of a Nazi. This whole interview is stupid. I don't want to be pressed into a mold. I am not willing to live out the fantasy of psychologists who see in me the twisted child of a Nazi big shot. I consider myself a human being responsible for her own actions. What I do is my own will and decision, and if that sounds ridiculous or pathetic, so be it. I never witnessed the Third Reich, I wasn't in the Hitler Youth, my neighbors weren't deported because they were Jews, I didn't amuse myself watching Jews scrub the sidewalks with toothbrushes. I never participated and I never looked away. I've never done anything to harm anybody. Am I an individual or a footprint in the sand? I must distance myself from you because you live in the past. I want to see as little as possible of you because your incompetence and helplessness get on my nerves. I can't help you, and I really don't want to. If I were to take the hand you're holding out asking for help you'd try to pull me down with you. You say you want to stand up, but you're afraid of your unsteady legs. I don't intend to lie down next to you. If you want to you can lie down in the mud, but don't let it rub off on me.

RAINER: For just a moment there I thought that we might become reconciled. But you're right, it's useless. Your way of dealing with weakness is in the best family tradition. The desperate are stepped on and the strong are praised. It's the well-tried system of praise according to ability, not need. It worked in the past and it still works with you. The proud, upright fighter who returns with head held high, even from prison, and who never was able to shed a tear over the disaster which he helped engineer. No hint of an apology, no admission of guilt, not a single word of regret. You can really be proud of that model, a father who manages a bank as matter-of-factly as an army, a universally valuable and useful man, except in situations demanding even a minimum of feeling and sensibility. Yes, he played games with me and read to me and consoled me when I scraped my knees when I fell off my bicycle. But what about later on when, full of dismay and inner doubt, I didn't know where I belonged? When his war crimes drove me, as you so aptly put it, from one camp to the other? When I tried to become a different German than he. Where was my father then? I had the unique opportunity of learning from someone who'd played a major role in the catastrophe. He could have explained to me why he had submitted, why he hadn't offered resistance, or at least why he hadn't called a halt in time. I heard nothing from him, not a word. And that's why I hate him, because in addition to messing up his life he missed the opportunity to let me profit from his experience. It might almost have been better if they'd executed him along with some of the others.

BRIGITTE: That's enough. I can't go on. Let's stop this conversation. It's pointless. Nothing in our relationship is going to change. On the contrary: our expectations of our father are diametrically opposed. I'm glad that he didn't burden me with stories about the past. I knew what had happened and I also knew about his role. What should he have told me? Having a father sit before me and confess his guilt? What a terrible thought. I can do without such a father, a father who weeps and feels sorry for himself, a father who whines and tells me about the mistakes he'd made. No thank you! Is that your idea of a historic opportunity? I'm glad that our father didn't do this, for I would have lost all respect for him. He settled matters within himself, and I am sure that it wasn't easy for him. After the defeat, while in prison, he had four years to think about where he'd gone wrong. Thank God he spared us. And in doing so he made our life easier, not harder. I don't see that as a negative. Of course he changed. After the war he no longer believed in National Socialism. He didn't join any of the rightist groups, and he steered clear of all those reunions of old Nazis. He became a true democrat. And that was enough for me. I didn't need any ridiculous admissions of guilt. He was capable of change, and that presupposes an awareness of having erred.

This has been terribly taxing, and now I'd like to stop. The real tragedy probably is the fact that my father's life elicits such disparate reactions. The catastrophe of the Third Reich and its collapse live on in our family. As a family we have failed. Everything you say and believe in is alien to me, as though you'd never been my brother. When I look at and listen to you I can't believe that we're the children of the same parents, that we grew up in the same house, that we played together when we were small. I am backing away from you. As a matter of fact, I really don't want to see you again. At times I feel that my little brother died long ago and that the man standing before me is a stranger. And often, when you talk about Father, I instinctively ask myself, "What does he know about my father?" And then I remember that he was your father as well. That may be the only thing I hold against him, the fact that his background is an obstacle to normal family relationships. As long as we live his fate will follow us, even though he died a long time ago and will be dead for even longer.

6

Susanne

The Hopeful One

JUST LOOK AT ME sitting here in front of you. My face, my eyes, my mouth, my nose. What do I look like to you? Tell me, what do you see? Suppose we were to run into each other at the supermarket on the check-out line. I turn around and you look at me. There's nothing special about me, right? And now here we are, talking about whether I'm the child of murderers —incredible! What does the child of murderers look like? Tell me truthfully, what did you think I'd look like? Did you have any mental image, any preconceived notion, what somebody like me would look like?

I was conceived in 1944, maybe at the very moment your grandmother was killed in a concentration camp. Or perhaps later that same day, after office hours. Father comes home from work and gets on top of Mother, probably after dinner. I really

The Hopeful One

don't know why I should talk about this with you of all people. But I have to begin with someone.

Actually, you're the first person willing to talk about it all. Probably this is going to turn into one gigantic agony.

We had some teachers at school who were willing to talk about it. One of them was an emigré who'd come back. He went to London with his parents in 1938, and he returned in 1945, hoping, so he used to tell us, to help in the rebuilding of a new Germany. He tried so hard to describe the horrors of the Nazi era for us. But all he accomplished was to make himself miserable, not us. When he talked about it he would tremble from head to toe and turn away to wipe away his tears. We sat there stoically, like Sunday at mass. All the pictures and films he showed us, the stories he told—they meant no more than anything else we learned in school. The bell rang, he came into the room, opened his briefcase, set up the projector, inserted the film, and the pictures appeared on the screen. He read from a book and showed us photographs. I was fourteen at the time. When the bell rang at the end of the hour we rushed out, ate our sandwiches, and got ready for our next class. And a few minutes later we were listening to our math teacher talk about straight lines and curves.

We were busy trying to solve math problems, not problems of history. It was all very meaningless.

In 1948 my father was sentenced to ten years, and he was released after two years, in 1950. I was three years old at the time he disappeared for those two years, and I never noticed it. I was five when he returned. I remember it like today. Suddenly he was there again. None of this was ever discussed at home. My father is still alive. He's almost ninety, a tall, proud man with a shock of white hair. His left hand is missing up to his wrist. He has an artificial hand covered by a black glove. It's inflexible and the fingers are slightly bent. He tends to extend his left arm slightly, as though about to shake hands. Strange, I always see this hand when I think about him. I don't see him as being evil. On the contrary. He never hit me, never yelled at me. He was calm and understanding, almost too calm.

"I'll tell you everything you want to know. Just ask me," he used to say to me, and invariably added this admonition: "And also tell your children. It must never happen again." He was making me responsible for the future, and it was up to me to shield my children against repeating his mistakes. The only problem was: What mistakes? All those historical revelations, those stories, were always so vague.

Mr. Stern—that was the name of the teacher who'd come back from London—once invited my father to school, and my father accepted. That morning he was very nervous. The upshot was that from then on the two met regularly at my father's suggestion. He was eager to see and talk to Mr. Stern. He was looking for understanding. And to this day I find it puzzling how he could talk so often and for so long with Stern, who after all had been one of his victims. When I was older he used to tell me: "We wanted to win at least this one war. We already knew in 1943 that we would lose the war against the Allies. But the Jews, they'd have to die."

He tried to explain it to me over and over again. Very calmly, no undue excitement, trying to win me over. He told me the story hundreds of times and made it all sound so simple and logical, even the most horrendous cruelties. Like stories about a vacation trip. Most of the time I just sat there listening, not saying a word. My thoughts tended to wander, or I would look past him out the window and think of something else. He talked in a soothing monotone, all the while looking at me, and I often felt that I was going to have to listen to him forever, for all eternity.

When I was sixteen he took me to Auschwitz. He knew the camp; he'd been stationed there at one time. We latched onto a German-speaking group. The guide was a former German prisoner. I'll never forget that day. There were many young people my age in our group, the only difference between them and me being that they were the children of victims.

My father didn't say a word during our guided tour. Later, in the car going back home, he began to tell me where he thought the guide had been wrong, which of his explanations were in error. He spoke about the selection at the unloading ramp and said that between 60 and 70 percent of the prisoners were sent to the gas chamber. The rest were put to work. It seems that the guide had said that all but a handful were exterminated immediately. And throughout it all my father was completely calm. And at the end he asked: "Can you imagine how horrible it all was?"

In retrospect, the terrifying thing about him was his objectivity. His reports and descriptions, his careful recapitulation of events. I never saw him shed a tear, never heard him break off in the middle, halt, unable to continue talking. Only these monotonous litanies, almost as though he were reading from a script.

I was raised by my father. I never knew my mother. She was killed in a bombing raid when I was a baby. Later we had a maid who took care of me and the household. He treated her very well. He was, as I already told you, a serene, friendly man. He believed that everything could be explained, and he followed his own logic. Once people were made to see the reasons why things happened, then all barriers to understanding and outlandish ideas would vanish. According to my father, everything that had happened back then was just a matter of cause and effect.

His father was an officer, and so he too became an officer. His parents were enthusiastic Nazis, and so he too became a Nazi. His entire family was involved in it from the very beginning. I never knew his father, he was killed in the war; he even knew Hitler. My father told me that in the early days, between 1930 and 1933, he often saw Hitler personally. "One couldn't resist the force of his personality," he used to say.

In his opinion the horror that unfolded during the war years grew out of the existing conditions and situations. However, in all honesty, my father never glossed over anything. He used words like "murderers" and "criminals." He never offered excuses and never claimed that the things we read about in the papers or books weren't true. But as to guilt, he never considered himself guilty. He never, not once, said that he had made a mistake or that he had been partner to a crime. He was simply a victim of circumstances. And I, I always believed everything he told me. I believed his assurances, believed him when he said that what happened had been a catastrophe, and I never suspected that he might be one of the guilty. But everything changed when my son demolished my view of the world. But more of that later.

After my graduation from high school, in 1962, I decided to study psychology, but later changed my mind and went into education. My husband and I met at the university. We married in 1965, and in 1966 I gave birth to my son, Dieter. Horst, my husband, teaches German and history.

One day about three or four years ago Dieter came home and told us that he had joined a study group to trace the history and ultimate fate of the Jews of our city. Wonderful, I said, and I was

proud of him. And Horst also said he would help him in any way
he could, with advice or books or whatever. Both Horst and I
were quite ingenuous and really proud that our son would un-
dertake something so important.

Dieter and his friends met regularly in the homes of one or
another's parents, including ours. They dug through the munic-
ipal records, wrote letters to Jewish communities, and tried to
find former residents of our city who had survived.

And then, after a few weeks, everything suddenly changed. I
began to feel uneasy. Dieter was hardly ever at home anymore;
every free minute was spent with his friends. And I was beginning to feel somehow that the more time he was devoting to his
project the more estranged he was becoming from us. He hardly
ever discussed his work with us; he stopped confiding in us and
became more and more secretive.

One evening at dinner—Horst and I tried to talk to him and
asked how his group was coming along—he suddenly looked up
from his plate, stared at me, and in a rather aggressive tone of
voice asked me: "Tell me, what did Grandfather actually do
during the war?"

I thought to myself, I'm glad that he's showing interest, he's
got a right to know what his grandfather did back then. And he
asked me to tell him what I knew. By then my father was in an
old age home, about fifty miles from here, and we visited him
once or twice a month, usually without Dieter. So I told Dieter
what I knew about those days, a past I knew only from my
father's accounts. I tried to explain, describe, interpret, and
report about a world which, as I now know, had nothing to do
with reality. My son listened to me for a while without looking
up. Suddenly he jumped up, threw down his knife and fork,
which he had been banging on the table while I was talking,

looked at me angrily, and shouted: "You're lying, he's a murderer! You're lying, you're lying! My grandfather was a murderer and is a murderer." He didn't stop until Horst got up and slapped his face. At that I began to scream at both of them. It was dreadful. Dieter ran to his room, slammed the door, and didn't reappear.

Something broke in that boy. Over and over again I tried to talk to him, to explain what had happened "back then," that damned "back then." I might just as well have been talking to the wall. He'd sit across from me, stare at my knees, wring his hands, and never answer. It was no use. He wouldn't listen to either of us.

Some weeks after that he came home, took some papers out of his bag, and threw them down on the table. They looked like old documents.

"Do you know a family by the name of Kolleg?" he asked. "No, never heard of them," I answered. "Here," he pointed to the papers in front of me, "they once lived in this house." "You mean, in our house?" I asked, trying to read one of the documents. "Yes, here, where we're living now," he said. I didn't know what he was after. "Yes, and what are you trying to tell me?" I asked. "Nothing important," he answered, and then went on very calmly: "The Kollegs were taken from this house in 1941, and in 1944 they died in Auschwitz. Your dear father moved into this house with your dear mother the day after they were taken away."

He then tore the paper out of my hand and shouted at me: "Do you want me to read it to you? Should I? Here, here it says, 'Here lived Martha Kolleg, age 2, Anna Kolleg, age 6, Fredi Kolleg, age 12, Harry Kolleg, age 42, and Susanne Kolleg, age 38. Arrested on November 10, 1941, deported on November

The Hopeful One

12, 1941. Official date of death of the children and mother, January 14, 1944. Father officially missing. Place of death: Auschwitz. Cause of death:—' Do you want any more details, Mother? And you want to tell me that you knew nothing of all this? Your father never told you any of this?"

I said nothing. I fidgeted, not knowing what to say to him. My father had never told me that we were living in a sequestered house. I assumed that it had been in the family all along. And damn it all, what should I have said to my son? Form an alliance with him against my own father?

I tried to talk to Horst about it, and he promised to have a talk with Dieter. But that didn't help matters. On the contrary, our son now also turned against his father. And Horst also didn't handle things very skillfully. He is a dedicated adherent of the Greens and considers himself a leftist. In his opinion our problems today, namely the ecology and atomic energy, are unique to our time. And he tried to persuade Dieter of this. The problem facing young Germans today, he insisted, wasn't fascism. The past was past and should be laid to rest. The critique of fascism was the province of philosophers, not teen-agers. Today young people ought to demonstrate against atomic plants, against the pollution of the environment. Everything else was socially conditioned and would have to await social changes, and then there would be no more fascism, and on and on with this theoretical twaddle. Dieter sat there, shaking his head, trying to get a word in edgewise, but Horst wouldn't budge.

Dieter finally gave up, but Horst kept talking. I tried to interrupt and asked Dieter how he now felt about it all. He looked at me, looked at Horst, and all he said was: "What on earth has all this to do with the fact that my grandfather was a murderer?" He then got up and went to his room.

SUSANNE

The next few weeks were horrible, nothing but arguments, fights, tears, and accusations. Dieter and I were on a collision course, like people of different religions and different truths. Horst took refuge in TV and refused to mix in, except that every now and then he surfaced with senseless advice—telling us to stop and not take things so seriously. But that wasn't of much help. On the contrary: Dieter took everything very seriously.

I feared that I was about to lose my son. I hadn't broken with my father despite all the stories he'd told me. But now a breach between me and my son became a real possibility. I found myself in the dreadful position of having to choose between my son and my father.

Before being forced into that choice I of course tried to reason with Dieter. We had not spoken to each other for about two weeks when one evening I asked him to listen to me one more time. I tried to make clear to him what my father had told me of his work, mentioned our trip to Auschwitz and other incidents of my youth. I wanted to make him understand what I'd been told of my father's past and of National Socialism, how I'd reacted to these accounts, and to what extent it affected my life, if at all. I also tried to make clear to him the difference between our two generations. When I was his age it would never have occurred to me to join a study group investigating the history of our town under National Socialism. Compared to today's youth we were stupid and naïve and uninterested, or possibly the subject was still too loaded then.

That conversation was very important. Dieter, no longer so resentful, listened to me very calmly and asked many questions. But I think the most important thing, as far as he was concerned, was my telling him that I was not going to defend my father at all costs, that his grandfather must not be permitted to come be-

The Hopeful One

tween the two of us, and that he must not think of me as an ex-Nazi clinging to faded ideals. I also made him understand that it is not all that easy to condemn one's own father as a murderer if one has never seen or experienced him in that role and if he had never shown me that side of himself.

Well, yes, basically what I did was to ask my son for forgiveness and, beyond that, for an appreciation of my situation. I left no doubt about my own rejection of the past and my father's deeds. That probably played a crucial part in our reconciliation.

In the days after our talk something wonderful happened to me. I forged a bond with my son—against my own father. Increasingly I began to take an interest in the work of his group, and he showed me everything he and his friends were collecting and digging up. His study group frequently met at our house, and I would sit quietly in the corner and listen to them. I was fascinated by the way young people today approach history. This generation is far less self-conscious and less fearful and inhibited than mine.

But this doesn't mean that everything was okay. I continued to visit my father every week, and every time before I went I planned to talk to him, but I never did. He had trouble walking, his hearing was bad, and I usually spent my time with him wheeling him around the garden of the nursing home. I simply couldn't get myself to ask him about the circumstances surrounding his acquisition of the house in which I now live.

I tried to persuade Dieter to come with me on one of my visits and to talk to his grandfather. He refused. "He's *your* father," he told me. I also thought that he would find a talk with his grandfather unpleasant.

Eventually I was able to persuade Dieter to come along. My father was happy to see his grandson. He hadn't seen him for almost a year. He asked him about school, and the two talked like old friends. I thought that perhaps Dieter had dropped his original plan. But I was wrong. After chatting about this and that Dieter came to the point.

He asked my father the same question he had asked me, namely, whether he knew the Kollegs. No, my father told him, he'd never heard of them. Dieter persisted and asked him how he'd gotten the house in which we lived. He bought it, my father told him. From whom? Dieter continued. From a real estate agent, my father answered. Did he know who had lived in that house before? Dieter asked. No, he didn't, my father replied.

And so the talk went back and forth without Dieter actually attacking my father. He asked him simple questions, and my father answered in his customary straightforward manner. I began to think that perhaps my father really didn't know anything. But Dieter, in his penetrating prosecutorial fashion, didn't let go, until my father lost his patience. "What is it you're trying to find out?" he asked Dieter. And so Dieter told him about his study group and the documents about the house they had dug up, about the proof of the deportation of the Kollegs, the people who had lived in our house.

But my father denied everything. He hadn't known it, he'd bought the house in the usual way; this was the first time he'd heard that Jews had lived in the house before him. Dieter didn't believe him, but he refrained from starting a fight with his grandfather. He whispered to me that it was pointless to talk to him about it. And we left it at that.

On that day my father died as far as I am concerned. I no longer know the man I continue to visit, and he's no longer of interest to me. We talk about meaningless things as I push his wheelchair around. Since that crucial visit we never again have

The Hopeful One

had a personal talk. I had found out that my father was a liar. And I didn't want to think about all the lies he'd been telling me all my life. Nothing was certain anymore, everything I'd been told may have been either half-truths or distortions.

Now I visit my father only once a month. Dieter has never again gone back with me, and I've never asked him to. I am now on his side and all my hopes rest in him. He is not influenced by my father's generation, and that's good. He is growing up far freer than I, and also far less in awe of authority. But the crucial experience in regard to my son is my alienation, with and through him, from my father. The old man living in that nursing home is a complete stranger to me. Someone else could be sitting in the wheelchair I keep on pushing around in the garden, and I wouldn't even notice it.

7

Gerhard

The Baffled One

IT'S GOOD to have a chance to talk to you about it here. Over the years my father's been accused of all sorts of things, and not one of them is true. Now I have the chance to straighten it out. Between 1940 and 1945 he was the mayor of this town. My mother was a guide in the BDM [League of German Girls]. My father's family were shopkeepers. His parents had a butcher shop, very small, nothing very much, just enough to support themselves. I still remember my grandparents. My mother also comes from here. She never really knew her own father; he died in World War I. He was a worker. My grandmother, that is, my mother's mother, took in sewing.

My father was born in 1910, my mother in 1914. As far as I know, both families have lived in this town for generations. My father is dead, and so is my mother. My father died in 1979, my mother in 1982.

My father joined the Nazis in the very beginning. I don't know exactly when, but he always said that he was in it from the start. That's where he and my mother met, at some party affair. Things must have been nice back then. Both of them were always so full of enthusiasm when they talked about it. Apart from his shop he gave as much time as he could to the party. He always said that he gave his all for his ideals. Mother was interested in the young people. She always liked children.

There were four of us children at home. Mother was always the most important person in our household. Father often got mad at us and also hit us, but in the end it was Mother who called the shots. I have two brothers and one sister. Stefan is the oldest one. He was born in 1936. Then came Gudrun, born 1939, and Anton, born 1941. I am the youngest. I was born in 1946, after the war.

Stefan became a plumber and now has his own business. Gudrun is a housewife, the mother of two; her husband works for the post office. Anton works in a garage; he's a foreman. I have my own butcher shop, not my father's old store. He sold his business when he went into politics.

I'm married and my wife works with me in the store. Our son, Gustav, is twelve, and goes to school. We're doing all right, except for the time when my father was involved politically, which later on was held against him. They kept on attacking him. After the war, long after he stopped being mayor, they kept going after him. Since he'd sold his business, he wanted to, actually had to, look for work, and that wasn't so easy. But thank the Lord the owner of the lumber yard—he'd always been on his side—hired him. They knew each other from before and helped each other when times got bad, just as my father had helped him when he was mayor. Thank God he was able to keep his lumber yard after the war and so could help my father. My father then became an executive in the business. That was good because it helped us get many things cheaper. After the war Father built a new house, and he also helped me with my shop. I now live in that house, and lots of the things in it are made of wood.

Mother stayed at home after the war. What with all the children she probably had to. She also took in sewing, just like her mother. For a while she tried to work in the kindergarten in town, but they didn't let her. Somebody there was sore at her. Why, I don't know. What did she do? Back then she played with kids and took them on hikes. What's bad about that? But probably some people revenged themselves in order to get some advantages.

Father didn't really have any difficulties after the war, except that he could no longer be mayor. The other political parties didn't nominate him, which meant that he also couldn't work in the town hall anymore. From one day to the next they took everything away from him. Long after the war he often said that the same people who'd given it to him took it away from him. I guess some were mad at him, but to this day I don't know why.

When I was little I was also blamed by some people. Your father was an old Nazi, one of the worst, a teacher once said to me. But thank God it was only that one teacher. He really hated me. When he saw me in a fight with another kid he'd yank me away and say what else could one expect of me. My father always said that he was nothing but an old Red who couldn't forget. He was a real enemy of my father. Even when they met on the street they didn't look at each other and didn't greet each other. Both of them looked the other way. According to Heinz, the teacher's son, my father was supposedly responsible for the teacher going to prison. Heinz is a year younger than I and was in the class below me at school, but not in the same school I went to, because he was the teacher's son. Our families lived near each other, but Heinz and I were never friends. He was angry, like his father. My father has hundreds of people on his conscience, Heinz once told me, and other crazy things like that. I got mad at him and told him to get lost, to leave me alone. He yelled back at me that I should ask my father what happened to the Jews here in town. So I asked my father, and he told me that they all emigrated to America and were doing all right there. They're probably better off there today than we are here. At least they weren't bombed and didn't have a war there. Years later some people from America actually came here, two old people and two young ones, about my age. And they came into our town in a big black Mercedes, walked around, and were received by the mayor. They didn't look like people who had everything taken from them. Only my father had everything taken from him. And they were welcomed and shown around, real guests. When talking about what things were like under the Nazis my father used to get really furious. When he heard talk about all the deaths and about the crimes of the Nazis on TV, he'd get very excited: "They always want to blame us for everything," he'd say. Or: "Lies, all lies." Or: "They always make us look bad, always only bad."

We children never really understood why he got so excited. But we knew that it was better not to talk to him about the war. And so we didn't. Mother used to tell us that at the beginning things were wonderful, but then they became terrible, and that we ought to be glad not to have been around then. My brother Stefan was already nine when the war ended. Stefan and

Gudrun used to tell me about the American soldiers who gave them chocolate. Stefan can remember the time when the Americans came. They were always so friendly; even when they came to pick up Dad they gave the kids chewing gum and chocolate. But Dad came back home soon. They couldn't do anything to him, he'd only been mayor.

Well, what else can I tell you? I've never been politically involved, and I don't belong to any party. It wouldn't have done me any good, they can't do anything for me. I'd rather not get involved. Yes, I vote, but I don't join anything, I mind my business. That's the only thing that interests me. Even though —and this sounds funny, because they've always criticized my father so—I might have had my chances. All of them, all the parties, often asked me whether I wouldn't like to become active. They even would have made it possible for me to get a seat on the city council. But my father was against it. He always said if they don't want the one, they shouldn't get the other one either. They wouldn't take him anymore, and so I didn't get involved.

Still, we often had a hard time of it. Once my father stopped being mayor we had many disadvantages. Look at Reimer, for instance, whose uncle later became mayor. He also has a butcher shop, and he got a location in the pedestrian zone— that's the best location in town. Everybody who passes by shops there. He's doing all right, selling prepared foods in addition to sausages and meat, and he's also gotten permission to put up three tables. And what did I get? This ridiculous little store by the road. Only because his uncle is a Red, and also the mayor. Do you call that justice? Is that the new town, the new times our teacher used to talk about, which began after 1945? What's the big change? And my father was also elected, just like the other one later on. Back then there was a majority for him, just as later there was another majority for the other one. I ask myself how could somebody elected by a majority be guilty? The upshot of all of this is that Reimer has his shop in the pedestrian zone and I don't. When I think of all the things I heard in school and on TV about the victims of the war. But it was always the other ones who were the victims. And what about us? Nobody talked about that. My father's brother, for example, was a prisoner of war in Russia and never came back. My mother's two brothers both died in the war. A half dozen of my father's relatives in Munich were killed in a bombing raid. We found out what war is like. Thank God, not I. But our whole family suffered under it. But they never gave us a penny, only the others. Who knows who all the people were who got things after the war, and what had really happened to them? What happened to us is clear: my father lost his job.

But there was a new beginning. Working together we helped in the reconstruction. Ten years later we again were a respected family living in a nice house, and Father again was respected in our town, even though not the mayor, but an executive in the lumber yard. And nobody said anything against him. Except the old teacher, of course.

Father always said we were a decent family. He was proud of his children and what they managed to achieve. Only he wasn't allowed to be mayor. And that's too bad, because maybe then I'd have a shop in the pedestrian zone.

8

Sibylle

The Orderly One

I ONCE READ somewhere that people have to be hugged three times a day to survive, six times to keep their feet on the ground, and twelve to grow. I think the people of my generation and that of my parents just got the minimum needed for bare survival, if that much. That's probably how things went on for hundreds of years, from generation to generation. My parents followed the educational methods of my grandparents, and who knows what I would have done had I had children. My father once told me that as a child he never was given the things he wanted, not even the most insignificant things. For example, he wanted to have raspberry soda with his meals, but as a matter of educational principle he never got it.

My three brothers and I also were subjected to a rigid fascist regimen at home. Hidings were routine. If I tore my dress—a beating; if I got poor marks—a beating; if I talked back to my parents—a beating. And if, as sometimes happened, minor transgressions piled up, then there too was a beating. The ritual never varied: we had to fetch the stick ourselves, lie down across a chair, and then it began. There was no point in trying to resist. And no back talk either.

Trying to talk our way out of it or persuade our parents not to hit us only made things worse. Mother was in charge of my punishment, and Father took care of my brothers. The only way out was not to get caught. That was an accepted, even approved method of avoiding the inevitable. As Father used to tell us: "Don't get caught."

Added to this there was the pecking order among the four of us, and so my older brothers also got into the act. I got it from both sides, from my brothers and from my parents.

I'll tell you why I call it fascist. Whatever self-respect we might have had was beaten out of us. They broke our will. Self-confidence and joy of life were trampled on in our family.

I still remember when I was little how sore I was at Little Hans, the boy in the nursery rhyme who cried when he got lost in the woods. Why, I asked myself, was he so eager to go back home? Just because his mother was going to be sad? I thought he ought to be glad finally to have gotten away.

All I ever wanted was to escape, preferably to a place where I didn't know anybody and where nobody knew how bad I was. I thought I must be bad, else why would my parents beat me? Recently I talked to my aging mother about these endless beatings. Unfortunately she hasn't changed. She still doesn't feel that she'd ever been unfair. Her only comment was: "If you'd behaved nobody would have punished you." And she added:

"Anyway, you liked it." I don't understand what she meant by that.

It took me a long time to break away from my parents. Only in the last two years have I begun to feel that I'm living free and independently. Before that things were very different.

When I was little I didn't react to the story of Abraham's sacrifice of his son the way other children did. I believed that parents had the right to kill their children. My father had also been the unloved child in his family. He had a brother two years older who died at the age of ten; he had been his father's favorite. Grandfather was in the steel industry. He was a heavy drinker and died young. My father also was in the steel business, and during the war he was stationed in Upper Silesia. He was exempted from military duty.

My mother comes from Magdeburg.* Her father had worked himself up and owned an oil-processing plant. Her brother was killed in the last days of the war.

Neither my mother's nor my father's family saw much inter-generational harmony. There was a great deal of fighting between parents and grandparents. Consequently I grew up without grandparents.

My mother was born in 1919. She met my father when she was quite young, about nineteen or twenty. At the time he already had an important job in the arms industry. He was a handsome man, tall, slender, and blond. They married soon after they met, and my brothers were born in rapid succession, 1942, 1943, and 1944. I was born in 1946, their only postwar child.

My father joined the SS right in the beginning, while still a

* A commercial center in Saxony.

student. He told me that he did things like ushering at meetings, and once he even was a bodyguard when Hitler came to Bad Godesberg. He said he wanted to make himself useful.

I wasn't actually all that interested in what he did during the war. I really believe that he didn't do anything. At least he wasn't connected with any concentration or extermination camp. What concerns me is what came afterward, the persistence of his frame of mind after the war. And his eternal sermonizing, that's what was so awful. He didn't let up until the very end, until maybe the last six months of his life when he got so sick.

Just a few days ago, in thinking about our conversation, I tried to pinpoint when I first learned about the crimes of the Nazi era in some detail. I think I must have been around twelve or thirteen. We had a priest who was preparing us for our first communion and he talked to us about it. At school we weren't told a word about anything. When I was thirteen I spent my summer vacation at a boarding school in Switzerland to learn French. Many of the girls there were American Jews. I remember how surprised I was by how friendly they were. I'd thought they'd ignore me.

At any rate, by then I already knew what the score was. But I didn't find out anything more specific until I was seventeen, when I visited relatives in East Germany, and for some reason or other we went to Sachsenhausen. The East German guides always tried to tell us visitors from the West that we were the ones who were responsible. We from the West were the evil ones; they hadn't done a thing. They were the better Germans.

They took us into the cellars and showed us the pictures of the Americans liberating the camp. Afterward I sat down by myself on the lawn outside and couldn't understand how it was possible for the sun still to be shining.

When I got back home I told my mother what I'd seen. Her only comment was: "The things you subject yourself to."

And it was just about then that my parents began with those speeches of theirs, or maybe my memory keeps harping on that time. The more I spoke about the past at school or at home, the more aggressive my father became: "That damn school, befouling their own nest. Things weren't that bad. And that business about the 6 million Jews, that's also exaggerated."

My parents had read Eugen Kogon's *The SS State*. In it he mentions a concentration camp doctor. It seems that my parents knew him, and according to them the day Kogon places him in the camp he wasn't there at all but at our house delivering one of my brothers. That was all the proof they needed to know that everybody, not only Kogon, was lying.

They always tried to minimize everything. The things that had happened were just accidents. No guilt feelings for them. The crowning touch was their cynicism in naming me Sibylle, having my first name begin with the letter "S," so that my initials now are SS. One of my father's little jokes, ice cold and unfeeling, making me go through life with that burden. I didn't think it very amusing. And when I said so, all they could say was that I had no sense of humor.

Our disagreements grew more and more heated the older I got. Again and again the question arose about how much they'd known and why they hadn't done anything about it.

And sometimes, very rarely, through hints, it became clear that they'd known everything. Once my father told me about waiting at the station at Eisleben* when a train with people in cattle cars pulled in. "Let us out of here," they cried. "They're

---

* A city in Saxony.

taking us to Theresienstadt." At that point he knew what fate had in store for these people. But when I asked him what he did about it, he got red in the face and shouted: "What did you expect me to do? With three young children. It's easy for you to talk."

After that I just gave up. I thought to myself, It's no use. Every argument we had about the Third Reich always went hand in hand with other prejudices which in the final analysis had nothing to do with the war. Jews and blacks were subhumans, and there was a whole catalogue of others he couldn't stand, like Indians and Greeks and Spaniards. And he never held back, regardless of where he was, whether in a neighborhood pub or among strangers. He also despised everyone who wasn't like him. He disparaged all who were too cowardly to speak their mind, even though, to hear him tell it, they agreed with him.

He was unsparing in his disdain. In 1967 I was on a Mediterranean cruise with him. It was the last time I spent a vacation in his company, one last attempt to share something pleasant with him. Half of the four hundred passengers were deaf-mutes, and that got him going. I was still stupid enough to try to reason with him. He cut me off by saying that he preferred two hundred deaf-mutes to two hundred blacks. Always that cynicism, that refusal to take me and what I had to say seriously. Things weren't as simple as I thought, I was illogical. One evening he got furious when I danced with an older man, a Jew, and jokingly said that I could imagine marrying someone like that. Yet when we landed in Israel two days later, he became enthusiastic about the uniformed young men and women in the harbor.

A year later, in 1968, came our final break. I turned Red overnight. In Bonn I'd fallen in love with a Communist, and he lent me a book by Ernst Fischer. Now for the first time I began to understand what was going on, and I promptly started to agitate. Of course there was a big row at home. Some weeks later I received a letter from my father. I had refused to spend Christmas at home with my parents. He exploded. He wrote he couldn't understand my extreme selfishness, couldn't understand why I bothered about blacks and Vietnam, that this riffraff was bound to disappear from the face of the earth without leaving a trace. I knew nothing about men, he said, and they don't like to have the things they'd created taken away from them. Men were proud, and I just didn't know what a real man was.

My mother added her signature to the letter. She agreed completely. Just imagine, all this happened nearly twenty-five years after the end of the war. And still that same language, that unchanged frame of mind.

After that letter everything was over. I became isolated, separated from the family. My brothers also knifed me in the back. They never had any problem with Father's past. And the fact is it was difficult to charge him with anything specific as far as the war was concerned. By sheer accident it seems that he was never present at any of the horrendous things that happened. And so he also had no problem with his de-Nazification. Yet a few months before the end of the war, when it seemed that he might be drafted, he wrote a letter to his oldest son, a testament of sorts, couched in the blood-and-soil phraseology typical of that era. I shudder to think that I'm related to its author.

My father remained a fascist to his dying day, and it really doesn't matter what he did or didn't do during the war. You can't imagine the beatings my brothers received. Once one of them was supposed to memorize a poem, and every time he stumbled Father let him have it. I can still hear the screams.

The Orderly One

Mother took me by the hand and led me out of the room. "Father's going to kill Erich. We better leave," she said to me. Things got really bad later on when we lived in our own house, with no next-door neighbors and no danger of being overheard. After that there was no stopping him. Given a choice I would never again live in a one-family house.

In my early twenties I tried to stand on my own two feet. But many of my own traits also frighten me, above all my lack of compassion. I think my greatest fear was that I would carry on the tradition of my parents and grandparents. I once saw a woman on the street hit her child, but I didn't intervene. I stood by and did nothing. And the real reason was that I didn't like the little girl. She just stood there and didn't defend herself, and that's why I didn't like her.

And later in the feminist movement, when I saw pictures of abused women, my instinctive reaction was: They had it coming, why didn't they defend themselves? If they'd defended themselves they wouldn't have been beaten. My compassion was reserved for people who defended themselves. My brothers and I also never defended ourselves when we were being beaten. We took everything, every conceivable humiliation.

But slowly I began to change. Years later I had a dream about a child that was being mistreated by other children. My first reaction in the dream was, well, they're only playing. I then saw them tie the child to a post upside-down and hit it on the soles with a stick. At that point I thought—still in the dream—these are torture methods. I went over to the child and intervened. That dream was a turning point in my life.

In 1973, six months after his retirement, my father died of cancer. When he became ill our relationship improved somewhat. We called a truce. At the very end he softened somewhat, becoming more gentle and sensitive. I spent much time taking care of him. My mother, on the other hand, paid him back for everything he had done to her. She treated him abominably and refused to have a nurse in the house. My father had intestinal cancer, and she really tortured him. She would give him an enema only if he was obedient. At the end things got so bad that his doctor insisted on calling in a nurse.

I was horrified by the way she treated that dying man. I moved back home, but it was a terrible time. I spent many sleepless nights.

Soon after my father's death I got involved with a man twenty years my senior. I now realize that he was just like my father—authoritarian, dogmatic, and domineering.

But now, after all those problems over the years, things have finally changed. I am living with a woman, and for the first time in my life I'm happy. I've given up the idea of emigrating. Three years ago I still toyed with the idea of going to South America and buying lots of land. But now that's all over. I'm even beginning to feel comfortable here in Germany; I realize that this is my home, despite or maybe because of everything that has happened here. I see all the ugliness, but also all the beauty, and I realize that I can't change very much, that nothing much has changed, and that it is possible that everything could happen all over again. The great pedagogic enterprises of the past twenty years haven't really changed the people. It can't be done by book learning alone.

I see that in the people I come in contact with. When one of my brothers was temporarily without a job he lashed out against everything around him—the foreigners, the unions, the workers—but as soon as he got a job again he became friendliness personified. The remnants of the past live on in all of us.

The Orderly One

The slightest disruption and we immediately take out after the others, always blaming others for our own inadequacies. Unfortunately I also see this trait in myself.

Sometimes I try to imagine what it would be like if I'd had children at my mother's age. I'm sure that I would have made them my victims. Now I'm glad that I don't have children and don't plan to have any. I don't want to be like my mother. I know that sounds absurd, but this distancing myself from her is important to me.

She hasn't changed. She's the same way she was thirty or fifty years ago. Once, when I told her about Viktor Frankl's book about Auschwitz, she said: "Oh, he must have been on the staff." She simply can't understand that an eminent doctor could have been an inmate in a concentration camp. The people in the camps were, after all, subhumans. That's what she believed then and that's what she believes still. She had a limited view then and she has a limited view now.

My parents were always—I'm sorry to have to put it so bluntly—limited, uninterested, and stupid. The terrible thing about them was their willingness to be manipulated. That, and their indescribable coldness. It's too bad, but I just have to talk about it. For years I tried to tell myself that they had a hard time, that they'd gone through a lot. Now I no longer have understanding for it. My father could have made a different choice, and so could my mother. At any rate, they could have done so after the war. After all, there's something like free will.

There was a time when I wondered how I would have acted in their place, and feared I might have been no different. But not anymore. I cannot relieve my parents of the choice they made. However, there's one thing I will never understand, what on earth made them decide to have four children.

SIBYLLE

There was a time when a reconciliation with my parents might still have been possible, but they missed the chance. If only once my mother had said to me: "Listen, I've thought about it, basically the worst thing we did was to close our eyes, and I will carry this guilt to my grave. But I hope you'll be different and learn from me."

I could have made peace with a mother like that, even if it turned out that she'd been a guard in a concentration camp.

9

Monika

The Believer

IT'S ONLY fairly recently, maybe ten years, that I've gotten up the courage to talk about my father being in the SS. Before that I didn't dare to. I always thought that if people found out they'd shun me, wouldn't want to have anything to do with me, that I'd be ostracized. And that's also how I saw my father, in the role of victim—alone, friendless, isolated—and I thought that's how I'd have to live for the rest of my life. And so I never told anyone.

And even now, when it comes to my father's past, I still get upset. He was in the Waffen-SS. Couldn't he at least have been in the SA [Storm Troopers], I ask myself. That would make it a little better; the SA wasn't quite so bad. Why the Waffen-SS? I never wanted to accept what he was really like. The mind may see things clearly, but the feelings refuse to accept what the mind sees. It's all very ambiguous.

My sister is older than I. I was born in 1947. About a year ago my sister suddenly announced that as far as she was concerned she was the daughter of an executioner. When I heard that everything in me recoiled. I thought to myself, No, I'm not like that, I don't want to be like that. But my sister hated my father, and she'd begun to delve into the past a long time ago. She says she simply has to live with the knowledge that she is the daughter of an executioner.

But I refused to see things in terms of black and white. I always tried to see both the good and the bad in people, and this desperate search for the evil that lies buried in the good, but also for the good within the evil, has always occupied me.

I studied psychology and after graduating got a job in a prison, working on an experimental program of alternative approaches to punishment. I was interested primarily in working with hardened criminals. I had good rapport with them and was completely unafraid. I often found myself in strange situations; big, powerful men, murderers and the like, would become violent, trash their cells, and no one would dare go near them. And there I'd be, the only one brave enough to walk into their cells and talk to them. I was never afraid of any of them. I started out from the premise that there's some good in even the worst, and that I was the one who'd find it. This ability to find the good in people was one of my strengths. The weakness of the strong, the goodness in evil, the soft core in hard people, that's what interested me, and that's what I was looking for in my father.

I refused to acknowledge that my own father had participated in all those crimes, and that's all there was to him. I also wanted to show him through my work that not all people in prison were alike. I wanted to prove to him—or maybe to myself—that I could find something of substance even in a thoroughly evil person.

But it was all in vain. He refused to listen to anything I tried to tell him. He was full of clichés: they were nothing but murderers and criminals, types who didn't want to work. It sounds crazy, but I tried to get him to understand criminals. No use. He was intolerant of the crimes of others and couldn't see anything good in any of these prisoners. It was a topsy-turvy world, for of course he never considered himself a criminal. And I kept on trying to prove to him that criminals were not born that way. But it didn't do any good, for he never saw himself in the same light.

We never talked about what he'd done. Silence and evasions were the rule. For years I knew nothing, unlike my older sister. She'd found out all about it. Certain subjects simply were taboo, and I didn't ask questions. I was obedient and didn't engage in discussion. I kept quiet.

That's how things went along until 1960, when I was thirteen, and my parents told me that Father'd been in the SS. For a long time after the war he lived under another name, probably quite unnecessarily so; he pretended to be my mother's brother. It was a crazy story, because my older sister also was told that he wasn't her father but her Uncle Franz. So for years we were a family in which a child was told that her father was gone but might still return from the war, and that the man living with them was her uncle. Of course my sister kept on waiting for her father to come back, and whenever there was an argument she'd say just wait till Daddy comes back.

Today my father's fear seems almost incomprehensible. On the one hand, I really don't know what he did during the war, but on the other hand I can't believe him when he says he hadn't done anything. Because if that were so, why did he hide for so long after the war, why was he so afraid that he pretended to be the uncle of his own child?

I can still remember the day my sister came to me and said: "Do you know who our father is? It's Uncle Franz." But I was still too young to understand it all.

At the time I learned about my father's SS past I was his favorite. And I loved him. I simply couldn't believe the things I was told about him. They had to be lies.

The explanation I was given went something like this: The SS was an elite unit of Hitler's forces which was always close to him and which fought for him, and that's why it is dangerous to talk about it.

Everything was shoved under the rug, everything was hidden: the uniform in the basement, the photographs in the linen closet. And always the fear that they might come and arrest my father. To this day I don't know of what or why he was afraid.

But all those disavowals, this hiding, this withdrawing, never leaving the house, never talking to outsiders, have left their mark on me. I remember one day I was walking home from school with some classmates when my father rode by on his bike. As he passed us he called out to me. One of the girls asked who that was, and I said that I didn't know.

I was torn. My father hid out, I hid him; he had no friends and spent his days riding his bike.

It took a long time for my anger against him to mount. Today I know that he'd always been a Nazi, and I no longer see two sides of him, only that one. The older I get the more I become aware of his aggressiveness and brutality.

Things he said that I'd forgotten or repressed keep coming back to me, such as his calling me a cripple when I was clumsy, or saying that I was lazy and that under Hitler I would have ended up in a labor camp. And then his anger, his screaming and rages. Never a calm sentence or a thoughtful answer. I've never once heard him say something positive about anybody. I can't remember him ever praising something or calling it beautiful.

Recently, not so very long ago, when he embarked on one of his tirades about the handicapped and other worthless lives, I called him a misanthrope. For the first time that I can recall he didn't flare up; he looked at me in astonishment and didn't say a word. Since then I've hardly spoken to him. I also told him that I was no longer willing to listen to his drivel. That hit home. For the first time. But it's taken me forty years!

The most important and most troubling thing for me is that basically I don't really know what he did during the war. Whenever I tried to get him to talk about it he dodged my questions, and if my mother was present she would intervene and ask why I keep harping on it.

The only times he gave himself away was when he got angry. A TV documentary about the Third Reich, a comment on the evening news about the Nazis, could set him off. "All lies," he'd shout. All reports and accounts of Nazi crimes were just a pack of lies. And it was during one of his rages that he mentioned for the first time that he'd lived in the Buchenwald personnel housing outside the camp. According to him the people who worked there were well fed and decently dressed, and they came from the camp. That, as far as he was concerned, was proof enough that all those stories about the concentration camps were lies.

And of course there were the Jews, his favorite topic. To hear him tell it they used to own everything, the big department stores, all the money, while the rest had nothing at all, nothing but poverty.

And today, as far as he is concerned, things are again the same. In America the Jews are in control, my teacher is a Red, and it's all propaganda.

He always denied everything. There were no murders, no extermination camps, and certainly no individual guilt. And these senseless outbursts always ended the same way: "One day you'll find out what really happened and then you'll thank me for always having told you the truth."

Yet despite everything, despite all these scenes, it wasn't easy for me to separate things into good and evil. I fought both against him and against myself. I taped some of my discussions with him and listened to them with one of my girlfriends. They always followed the same pattern, always the same phraseology and the same aggressions. I tried to argue with him calmly and logically. For years I kept on trying, never giving up. It's only now that I begin to realize how senseless it all was.

I once had a boyfriend who also was pretty aggressive. He used to shout at me, and when he did I couldn't think straight; my mind became a blank. Just like with Father. I keep on looking for men who aren't aggressive.

As I grew older I began to edge away from my family. I realized that people like my father couldn't be changed or convinced. And so the only solution for me was to get away from home. I stopped bringing my friends to the house. I moved out after finishing high school, and my visits became rarer and rarer. There were big emotional scenes. My parents' favorite saying was that blood was thicker than water. That was supposed to mean that there was something like family solidarity, and that it outweighed anything else. What they didn't see was that this sham closeness was the very thing that had driven me away. They couldn't forgive my sister for not inviting them to a birthday party with her friends. Our so-called family was supposed to take precedence over all others.

It's hard to believe that for years I kept on worrying about it, that I didn't simply turn my back on them and walk away. I took everything they said seriously, and I was taken in by it. But in the final analysis, the pretended warmth, the pleas, the stress on family ties was nothing but a sum total of regulations and norms, not of personal values.

Mother was given to saying that one had to be good, and that good people had no bad sides. It was that simple. And in her eyes Father had only bad traits and no good ones. Yet despite their squabbles they're still living together. They have nothing but contempt for each other but keep up the pretense of being a close-knit family.

They also made me into a nice little girl—noble, helpful, and good. No anger, no troublemaking, no irascibility, and too little resistance to parental authority.

But I hadn't always been like that. When I was small I was a little witch who later changed into an angel. I used to throw tantrums, stamp my foot, and fight back. But then sometime later, about 1960, around the time I learned of my father's past, everything changed. At around the age of fourteen I became gentle and kind and obedient, always smiling. I liked myself in the dual role of witch and angel, switching from one to the other. The older I got the more determined I became to show the world how sweet and good I was, never angry. And I'm still like that, even though it bothers me.

Nice people don't fight back, don't raise their voice, and would never admit that something makes them mad. That's how I was brought up. I've been housebroken.

There came that ominous moment when I stopped defending

myself. With one stroke they broke my will, supposedly with love. Mother was always so disappointed when I became angry, and then promptly forgave me. She said she'd forget that I'd been so bad. Double torture.

Finding out about my father's past, the deception, the recognition that he wasn't the kind, good person I had thought, also affected my feeling of independence. I changed, became shy and anxious. I also cried a lot, and when I did I'd go down to the basement, sit down on a crate, put on my father's old uniform coat, and stay there until all traces of tears disappeared. I still find it difficult to assert myself, to say what I want and what I don't want. I have inherited much from my parents.

My greatest problem is to avoid becoming like my parents, given their past. I know what I have in common with them. And I wasn't able to change, to make myself over, until I stopped thinking of them as victims. I also saw myself as the victim of their upbringing and their past. But as soon as I stopped seeing my parents as victims I became able to distance myself from them. Having looked at the historical record, the books and films, I have become convinced that they must be counted among the perpetrators. But when I was small, as a child, I saw something altogether different. They were refugees with very little money, frightened people living from hand to mouth. That's not what perpetrators are supposed to look like. They saw themselves as victims and felt like victims, and that's how I saw them as well. And I also began to see myself as their victim. I now know that what they did is also a part of me, but I now handle it differently, and that is the beauty of my life today.

10

Herbert

(A Telephone Conversation)

PETER S.: *Have you come to a decision about talking to me?*
HERBERT: No, I haven't.
Why not?
I don't know what you want to know.
I'm interested in your parents.
Why?
Good question.
There's not much to tell.
Well, let's begin with the little there is.
What do you want to know?
Everything and the truth.
Where should I begin?
Wherever you can.
I don't think I can at all.

What?

Talk about my father.

Why not?

Because you probably want to hear that he was a criminal.

Well, was he?

You'd call him that.

What do you call him?

I call him Father.

And what else?

What do you mean "what else"?

What was he before he was your father?

How should I know?

Why don't you ask him?

Why?

Maybe he was a criminal before he became your father.

Are you trying to insult him?

Maybe.

You don't have the faintest idea who he really was.

True.

He was a soldier like thousands of others.

A soldier in Treblinka?

In a *Sonderkommando.**

What kind?

In the office.

That's what he told you?

Yes.

When?

A long time ago. When I asked him what he did during the
war.

---

* The "special detail," a euphemism for the extermination squads.

(A Telephone Conversation)

How old were you at the time?

I think about fifteen.

Why did you ask him?

We'd talked about the Third Reich in school.

What else did he tell you?

That sometimes he also guarded prisoners.

What kind of prisoners?

The ones that were held there.

Who were they?

Don't ask such stupid questions.

Can't you say that word?

Which one?

What kind of prisoners they were.

Okay, Jews.

Why are you shouting?

You get on my nerves.

So?

I'm going to stop now.

All right, hang up.

Okay.

What did he do with the Jews there?

He didn't kill them, if that's what you mean.

Then what did he do?

Guard them.

How did he do that?

He didn't tell me every little detail.

What did he tell you?

He wasn't in the gas chambers.

Where was he?

In the office.

And that's where he guarded the Jews?

Don't be so aggressive.

Are you surprised?

What do you and I have to do with it?

Not much, except that maybe your father killed my grand-mother.

That's ridiculous.

I'm not laughing.

There's nothing he could have done.

What couldn't he have done?

Refuse.

Why not?

Because then they would have killed him.

Who's "they"?

The SS, of course.

But he was in the SS himself.

But not voluntarily.

That's what he told you?

Yes.

Who forced him?

I don't know exactly.

Didn't you ask him?

Get off me. It wasn't my fault.

It wouldn't be if you'd asked him.

He wanted to survive, that's all.

By killing others?

He didn't kill anybody!

You don't believe that yourself. He was there for three years.

He was in the administration.

That makes him a desk murderer.

It's terrible, the way you talk about him.

How do I talk about him?

(A Telephone Conversation)

Like a common criminal.
Well, and?
But he's my father.
So?
Hundreds of people worked in the administration there.
In that case there were hundreds of murderers.
You're bitter.
That's true.
I ask myself what do I have to do with all this?
Nothing.
Then why do you attack me?
Because you're protecting your father.
Do you want me to attack him?
Makes no difference to me.
What do you want me to do?
Find out the truth.
And when I do?
Then attack him, if that's what he deserves.
My own father?
If he was a criminal then tell him so to his face.
My own father?
I feel sorry for you.
What do you mean by that?
You're pitiful.
Why?
With a father like that.
You're insulting him again.
I don't like him.
But you don't even know him.
I know enough about him.
But he also has a very different side.

Which one?

He can be kind and friendly and nice; and also funny.

What's that got to do with it?

Damn it, you have to deal with your hatred yourself.

And you?

I don't hate him.

He's a murderer!

There you go again.

I'll never stop.

Can't you forget?

Some things, no.

Neither can he.

Poor guy.

He went through a lot.

Like what?

He was persecuted and tried after the war.

Yes, I know, and he was acquitted.

As he should have been.

How do you know that?

I believe him.

What? That he didn't do anything?

Yes.

You're lying to yourself.

And you with your hatred also aren't bringing anyone back to life.

I'm not so much interested in your father as in you.

How come?

How you can live with it.

I'm not living with him now.

Do you love him as a father?

No.

(A Telephone Conversation)

When did you stop loving him?
  I never loved him, but I respected him.
And now?
  Now I only feel sorry for him.
Why?
  He's old and shaky and can't walk without help; he can't even
  feed himself.
Why didn't you love him?
  Maybe I even hated him.
Do you feel indifferent about him?
  No, not that.
Are you different from him?
  Yes and no.
What do you mean?
  There's too much of him, things I don't like, in me, and vice
  versa.
And what else?
  Nothing.
Tell me more about yourself and your father.
  Leave me alone.
Do you find our conversation unpleasant?
  Yes, very.
Why?
  You have an unpleasant way of questioning.
You think so?
  You're pushing me over to his side.
I don't want to do that.
  But you are.
With you and me there are no two sides.
  And in my father's case?
There they exist.

And you are pushing me in that direction.
I didn't want that.
You're using guilt.
How?
If I don't hate him I share in the guilt.
No, no.
Oh, yes. You're making it easy for yourself.
No, that's not what I mean.
Oh, yes.
What am I doing wrong?
You're playing a nasty game.
Now you're going too far.
You're going too far with your hatred.
I don't understand.
I can't help your hatred.
I know that.
That's why you'll be left with your hatred.
How come?
Because I won't help you.
And I don't need you.
I doubt that.
Why?
I can forget, but you can't.
You've already said this.
Now I feel sorry for you.
Thanks a lot.
You're the sorry creature.
Now just a moment!
You're desperate, like a dog who barks and nobody hears him.
You can kiss my ass.
Nobody will help you.

(A Telephone Conversation)

Forget it.

Your hatred will consume you, but I'll live.

Lots of luck to you.

Ridiculous, the way you're carrying on.

That's brave talk on the part of the son of a hangman.

You can't insult me.

I know that.

Let's stop. This doesn't make any sense.

Yes, let's stop so that you can bring that old shit his hot tea.

Now you're going too far.

Yes, you're right, let's stop.

There's nothing more we can say to each other.

Alas, yes.

I'm not going to give you any interview.

I no longer want you to.

You don't ask questions. All you do is swear at people.

That's true, at least in your case.

Too bad, because maybe we missed an opportunity.

Maybe you're right.

Does that mean that we're now enemies?

Of course not.

What then?

I don't know.

Actually, it's all very sad.

Yes.

Do you really think my father is a murderer?

I no longer know.

I just can't imagine it.

Neither can I.

It's mind-boggling.

You're right.

All right.
Yes.
I don't think I'll give you that interview.
As you wish.
Are you sorry?
No.
Neither am I.
I believe you.
I wish you luck.
So do I.
Maybe we'll run into each other by accident.
I don't even know what you look like.
That's true.
Well, lots of luck.
Yes, to you, too.

11

Egon

A Dweller in the Past

THE DAY AFTER finishing high school I told my mother that I was going to study medicine. I think it came as a shock to her. She looked at me, very frail and shaky, and only said: "Child, please don't do this to me!"

She just didn't want it. Under no circumstances. I told her that there was no use in arguing, that I'd made up my mind that I wanted to become a good doctor like my father. Never mind what he'd been charged with.

Mother just didn't want to believe me. She was unhappy, cried, mumbled to herself. I couldn't understand a word, but I guess that was just as well. I didn't really want to hear what she had to say. I knew that whole litany, that my father, because of his profession, had brought nothing but misery on the family. It's been a bone of contention for years.

EGON

Father's profession wasn't a disaster, nor what he did and for whom he did it. And at the time my mother didn't object. She was young and probably didn't mind being the respectable wife of the young SS doctor. But all of a sudden, when things came crashing down, and it became a crime to have been involved, Father alone was supposed to be responsible for the misfortune of our family. Ridiculous. My father was a physician and scientist and a dedicated National Socialist.

Mother maintains he didn't have to volunteer for Dachau in order to make himself useful. But at the time she was glad that he didn't have to serve at the front. And all she does now is complain that he would have spared the family much unhappiness if he'd just remained an ordinary doctor. There wouldn't have been all those troubles after the war, but he had to mix into everything, be part of everything. That's all I hear day in, day out, year after year, particularly since his death. When my older sister is here, she's sixteen years older than I and was born during the war, the two of them join forces. They really get me mad, trying to put all the blame on Father. If only he hadn't, if only he had. Father died six years ago, and he's been dying daily ever since. They won't let him rest in peace. The fact that my sister, Susanne, is on her third marriage—all his fault, the way he brought her up. Moreover, with his past he didn't set her a good example, except negatively. I guess it's all an attempt to put distance between him and herself. I don't know what all that is supposed to mean. He's dead. How much distance can she put between him and herself? That Mother can't make ends meet —his fault, because he didn't leave enough and couldn't get a decent position after the war. That I'm so hard to get along with—his fault, because he never paid any attention to me. I think they also blame him if they get constipated.

A Dweller in the Past

But when he was still alive there wasn't a peep out of them. It was Daddy this, and Daddy that, and aren't you too tired, and don't you want to rest, and bring Daddy the paper and slippers, and how do you like the soup, and did you have a hard day. Susanne hugged him when he came home from the office, and Mother kissed him on the cheek, but with clenched lips. When I was little I was struck by the way they kissed, never really touching each other with the lips. When my mother hugged me I felt disgust. She'd press her clenched lips against my cheek, and I felt the few hairs on her upper lips brush my skin. I shuddered when she caressed me.

When we went out for a walk Father would walk in the middle, my mother and my sister to either side of him, arms linked, moving in unison, with me tagging along. The three of them ignored me. My mother and sister hated him, I worshipped him, but he was indifferent toward me. Unbelievable. When he played with me he was just doing his duty. When I showed him something he didn't see it, even if he was looking straight at it. He forgot my birthday and hundreds of promises to play with me or go biking with me.

And I admired him so, and defended him whenever anybody tried to besmirch him. I was a child of his later years, an unwanted child. Actually everything that makes for a family was already destroyed by the time I was born, in 1960. At the time my father was fifty-six, my mother thirty-eight. My sister was born in 1944. My parents met in the camp, but of course not as prisoners. Quite early in the war my father returned from the front with a leg injury, which left him with a permanent limp. It wasn't a battle wound but the result of a car accident. There was something fishy about it. Perhaps he was drunk. At any rate,

after being released from the hospital he volunteered for Dachau. That's what he told me.

My mother was the daughter of one of his colleagues. I don't
know what more I can tell you. He joined the National Socialists
in the very beginning, as a student in Berlin, back in 1933, when
they tried to prevent the Jewish students from entering the
university and took their IDs from them. He used to tell me
about it. On graduation from medical school he immediately
joined the SS. He often said that the doctors kept faith with the
party from the very beginning. Rumor even has it that the
Voelkische Beobachter, the official paper, was given to the party
by a group of doctors. He was proud of his role in the war to the
very end. His favorite saying was that doctors protect and pro-
long the lives of people. Doctors who are nationalists do that, if
need be even at the cost of the lives of others. That, he said, was
the difference between a doctor who has political convictions
and one who doesn't.

He believed that it was his duty to help and work "selec-
tively." He did not think that all lives were equally valuable. He
did not, like some others, become an SS doctor in order to
advance his career. After all, enough places had opened up
through the expulsion of Jewish doctors. He despised these
careerist toadies, and he also blamed them for the catastrophic
end of the movement.

He used to say that basically all people act the same, except
that some actions are justified and others aren't. Take a soldier
and a murderer. Both kill. But one is honored and the other is
executed. When he talked like that I would sit there and just
listen to him. He didn't tolerate interruptions or interjections.
Perhaps he wasn't even aware that I was listening. He considered himself part of the elite of the Third Reich, an individualist

A Dweller in the Past

in the mass movement. In his eyes the German nation was an organism, a body, and as a doctor it was his duty to shield that body against sickness and disaster, to remove the diseased part and to conduct research to prepare this body for the future. That was his constant refrain.

What a feeling it must be, being responsible for millions of people, yes, for the future of the entire German nation. At the time he was very young, barely older than I am now. What, I ask myself, do I have to show? To be entrusted with such tasks—what more can a young scientist ask for? Say what you will about National Socialism, but basically it rested on a philosophy of medicine. Concepts like race, nation, living space, race hygiene, race preservation, and race philosophy are unambiguous. No new society can be built without doctors. These conclusions largely reflect the views of my father.

I'm certainly not a neo-Nazi. I don't even know what that's supposed to mean. Those days are gone, and you'd have to be stupid to want to see them return. It would mean that I'd also want to see a replay of the defeat. The system failed not in its ideas but in its execution. Well, maybe in some of its ideas, but not in the basic ones. I always spoke up when I heard the Nazi era being indiscriminately attacked. At school I was often the only one to get so involved. We had a history teacher who called himself a confirmed antifascist. But he'd been just a child during the war. Now, when fascism no longer exists, it's easy for him to be against it. It doesn't affect his life. At first I used to keep quiet at school, thinking to myself, Let him talk, I know what I know. But it got worse and worse. If what he said was true, we Germans were a nation of criminals and madmen. And we now know that's not so. Our former enemies have become our closest allies.

EGON

Once we had to write a composition on the topic "The Role of the Medical Profession in the Crimes of National Socialism." I said to myself, That's it. I'm not going to let them run my father down. I wrote a paper defending the doctors, using the arguments I'd heard from my father. You can't imagine what happened then. I was called to the principal, and so were my parents. They threatened to expel me, to report my parents to the authorities, and I don't know what else. But they could find no arguments to counter mine. They accused me of being a neo-Nazi. That was odd. A few years ago you probably couldn't even become a postman without belonging to the party, and now membership in it is a term of abuse. Then they tried to catch me with all sorts of sly questions, whether I had feelings about the Turks or belonged to any organization or had painted swastikas on walls. I decided to keep my mouth shut, and I did. I didn't say a word. Only when they asked me whether my father was behind it all did I become mad. I had a mind of my own, I told them. Then I shut up again. There were the usual reprimands from the principal's office and the matter was dropped.

One evening my father had a talk with me, maybe the only time in my life that he spoke to me calmly and not past me. He looked straight at me, man to man. It was wild. And he wasn't mad at me. On the contrary. He tried to explain to me that nowadays opinions like mine can't be aired openly. He criticized me, but I had the feeling that he was proud of me.

After the war he could no longer work as a doctor. Some friends offered him a job in the pharmaceutical industry, and that's what he did until his death. He also changed his profession. When people asked him what he was he told them he was a research chemist. I think he was ashamed of being a doctor who wasn't practicing medicine.

A Dweller in the Past

We always lived in Berlin. That's where I went to school. I expect to be finished with my studies soon and plan to specialize in internal medicine. That's what interests me most. My sister also lives here in Berlin. She's a teacher. She's been married twice before, once even to a Jew. The things she's tried and experimented with! I am very different. We've lost touch with each other. I look forward to the day when I don't have to see Mother or her anymore.

We see each other only at Christmas. And even then she starts on me. I no longer react. Soon after entering medical school I joined a student group dedicated to the protection of Germanhood. We try to preserve the positive aspects of the past and to prepare for the future, to make us proud once more of being German. We meet every Tuesday. But we are not a dueling fraternity. That's not for us. We don't want to live in a museum, and we are not museum custodians. We're mainly concerned with creating a new national identity, a German nation that is proud, without resorting to a dictatorship, at least not one like National Socialism. Back then it was important to prevent Communism, or by now we would probably be part of the Eastern bloc.

Too bad that Father talked so little of those days. He was a very quiet person. In all those years he told us very little of his work at Dachau, except for an occasional remark about experiments, or the treatment of inmates, or about the death of thousands, or the sudden collapse, which no one in the camp expected.

Would I have acted the same way then? I think so. It was war and everybody was so enthusiastic. And the war was fought not only at the front between two enemies, it was also fought at home. The enemies were not only Russians or Americans, but also Communists, Jews, and Gypsies. Is that so absurd? There is something absurd about every enemy, every hostile person. Someone is standing in front of me, a man who looks exactly like me, and suddenly he's my enemy.

I either believe that or I don't. And if I believe it, then I accept the idea of an enemy. An enemy soldier or an enemy race. That was the ideology back then. I don't understand why we now see this in such a different light. Why should a soldier who for years had shot at people, thrown hand grenades into buildings, sunk ships, dynamited bridges, killed women and children, be allowed to return home after the war and to live in peace, while my father is considered a criminal? Both were ordered to kill, each in his way. Both were convinced that what they were doing was right.

As I've already told you I would have acted the same way. I can imagine that this disturbs you. But I'm not going to stand here as a man who denies his father. On the contrary, I'm proud of him.

For years he lived with the awareness that he might be indicted, but he wasn't afraid. I admired him, but he ignored me. That's really the bad part of his story. Those scenes at Christmas, terrible. He'd spend hours with my sister unwrapping her gifts, admiring her as she tried on her new clothes and necklace. He adored her and ignored me. He was never unkind and he never hit me. Only his looking past me, that's what was so terrible. When I talked to him I had to repeat things three or four times before he reacted. Why? I just don't know. He hated his own son, or at the very least was indifferent toward him.

My mother keeps telling me that I look exactly like he did when he was young. Shortly before the end of the war he fled to

A Dweller in the Past

Berlin. Afterward, when everything was over, he went on living like everyone else.

At the moment I don't know what to do. Everything is so confusing. Sometimes when I talk about him I feel as though he were a stranger I'd never laid eyes on but knew from hearsay. And so I pass on the things I've been told, not my own impressions. If you were to ask me today what he looked like I'd have to look at a picture to bring him to mind. What color were his eyes? Blue, I think, but maybe gray. He was stocky, not very tall, a little pudgy, a little like myself. We're no beauties. My sister also isn't very attractive. Maybe that's why she has such problems with men. I don't have a steady girlfriend now and never did. I once dated the daughter of friends of my parents, but it didn't last long. I have problems with today's women. How should I describe it? They don't interest me. Maybe I should try it with an older one. The young ones and those my age don't understand me. And the things that interest them don't interest me. I'm dreaming of a real companion, someone who'll stand by me through thick and thin. And, of course, political agreement is also important. But there are hardly any women in our group, and those few are already taken. But I suppose somebody is bound to come along eventually. There are plenty of women around, so I guess I'll find one.

No, I'm not afraid of them, that's not it. But when I see all these young men chasing after women, I prefer to hang back. My sister had a succession of men. She even brought them home and spent the night with them. She has no shame. But it doesn't do her any good. She's as lonely as I. I'd rather wait.

I do have friends. My comrades. They stick by me. We all

stick together. When one of us needs help we're all there. No fear of being left stranded.

Two years ago I moved away from home. I rented a room from the widow of a friend of Father's. She has a huge apartment and lives alone. She also looks after me, prepares my breakfast and does my laundry. Actually I'm very well taken care of there, better than at home. Also she likes to talk about the past. She knew my father before the war. I think her husband was also a doctor. From her I found out what my father was like when he was young, how he looked, how he met my mother, and also some details about his work during the war. She also told me that my father enjoyed a good reputation also among the prisoners. He wasn't one of those slaughterers, one of those murderous sadists. These labels are also too simplistic. It's even said he helped some prisoners escape, but maybe that's just a rumor.

My landlady has a daughter who's a little older than I. She lives in another city, and once a month she visits her mother. What happens on these occasions I can tell you only if you promise not to mention any names. I'm no Casanova, but when she visits she sleeps with me. She just comes into my room, lies down in my bed without much ado. Nothing like that's ever happened to me before. And her mother knows about it but doesn't say anything. Maybe she hopes that I'll marry her daughter. I've thought about it, but I fear she's a rather loose young woman. Does she do the same thing with other men? I ask myself. She is so shameless that I have to admire her. Completely uninhibited, always laughing and cheerful. When I tell her of my worries she just laughs. And strangely enough, my worries then don't seem quite so overwhelming anymore.

Perhaps one day we'll become the new elite. I'm certain that times will change and some aspects of the past will return. Things will be different, but they will also be different than now. People can't live without symbols and leaders, at least not in the long run. The new leaders will be different. The goal won't be war or the destruction of others, but power without war. Survival won't be predicated on the death of others. There will be sovereignty without victims, but through subjugation, positive subjugation. Nowadays it's no longer so simple to mobilize the masses. People have become more critical. And critical people can be stirred up only if they have an enemy who corresponds to their critical consciousness. The peace movement has demonstrated this. We've studied it closely. It proved that Germans can still be mobilized, only it's got to be the right enemy.

My friends and I—most of them are doctors—are ready. We have time. Unlike our fathers, we won't let any old idiot use us. As doctors we're indispensable to any political change. The nation, being a living entity, needs doctors. If need be they can also kill, not out of joy in killing but out of necessity. It's part of the job. Just as a doctor can save the life of a patient by removing an appendix he can save the body politic by excising big tumors. The extinction of life also forms the basis of the survival of others. This is where personal conviction comes in. My father serves as a model in this respect.

I know who you are, and I can imagine how you now feel about me. But I am an honest man and I don't want to pretend to be something I'm not. The matter is too important for that. My father killed, yes, that's true. Maybe he has hundreds of inmates on his conscience. He conducted experiments on people, he failed to help sick prisoners, and he did nothing to bring down the death rate in the camp. But keep in mind: whatever he did he did out of deeply held convictions, not out of a lust for

murder. He wasn't a pervert but a political animal who acciden-
tally found himself on the wrong side. If not for that he would
probably have retired as a highly respected professor instead of
spending the rest of his life after the war hiding out as a chemist
in a research laboratory.

I will do things differently yet without being different.

12

Ingeborg

The Conciliator

I WAS BORN in 1945 in Carinthia [Austria]. My father is also from Carinthia. He comes from a poor family. After World War I his father made his way from a prisoner-of-war camp in Siberia all the way back to Carinthia. That must have been quite a trip. But somewhere in the Slovenian region he was recaptured and was beaten so badly in prison that he died of a ruptured kidney. That probably made my father into a German national-ist. His mother was then left to fend for herself.

I once went to look at the house in which he grew up—a one-room stone cottage alongside a brook, with only a little stove to heat it. It was a kind of poverty which today seems almost unimaginable. Winter and summer my father went around in wooden clogs without socks. The bread spread was beef fat, and his mother earned a few pennies doing sewing for the local farmers.

That also explains my father's dislike of Catholicism. The farmers with whom he had to stay mistreated him terribly, but on the outside they were pious. My father was very athletic and daring. He once did a handstand on a factory smokestack and walked across a river on the railing of a bridge, and many other stunts like that. I heard lots of such stories about him. But as I mentioned before, always that dreadful poverty. He told me that he used to look into the window of a local candy store and dream about one day being able to buy all those wonderful things there. Those were his fantasies.

Maybe it was through his sports club, or maybe he was fired by the idea of a German national purity and ethic, I don't really know, but he joined the National Socialists very early. He was always politically naïve, but that movement must have fascinated him. He was a so-called Illegal,* and long before the Germans marched into Austria he was sentenced to two years.

When he was released he immediately went to Germany. The mass movement there inspired him. He was accepted at the sports academy in Berlin and finished the course successfully. That must have been his finest hour, before the war in Berlin, when the Olympics and the entire fascist movement were at their height. He personified the National Socialist ideal— young, wiry, clean, fanatical, and without any doubts. He then returned to Carinthia and became something like a regional athletics chief, opened a sports academy, and was very active in the party organization.

* The National Socialist party was officially banned in Austria between 1934 and 1938.

The Conciliator

When the war broke out Father immediately volunteered. He could have been exempted, but he didn't want that. He believed that one couldn't let others fight for one's ideals. He served in Poland and Russia. That's all I know about that. From what he told me he always fought alongside his men on the front lines. At the end of the war he returned to Carinthia and hid out from the British in the mountains. They were looking for him. I never found out why. He was said to have been decorated with something like the Order of the Blood. Toward the end of the war he served in Italy and was supposed to execute partisans. He told me that he refused. But how he got from the Eastern front to Italy and then back to Austria, and the whole business with his decoration, I don't really know.

I was born in 1945. He sent the British word that they could stop looking for him and that he would turn himself in after the birth of his child. Which he did.

The British sentenced him to two years, and he served the full term. A few years ago when I visited Israel with my husband, Alex, we ran into a relative of Alex's who'd worked in the prison where my father was interned. I must say that was a strange situation for me. You know that my husband is Jewish. But more about that later.

When I was around seventeen or eighteen I began to stand up to him. There were two topics: the Nazi era and the Jews. I wanted him to be critical of the past or talk about his mistakes. But he was defensive. He simply wasn't ready to bad-mouth the commitment of his youth.

When the talk turned to Jews, he naturally got to Israel: "Just look what they're doing in Syria today and with the Palestinians." And then came all those unbelievable clichés about the Jews being just as militaristic and sticking together, that we are the only ones who are so self-critical, that they can do whatever they please, and so on, and so on.

And then one day he told me that when he was in prison he was beaten by a British Jew who screamed at him and called him a Nazi swine. That was supposed to prove that they weren't any better. I tried to tell him that this sort of personal anger couldn't be compared to the crimes of the Nazis, but it was useless. Taking on such a father wasn't all that simple. When I still lived at home we were an ideal family. Father was very family-minded; he didn't drink, didn't smoke—no vices. Sports were important; we hiked, sang, and always did everything together.

If only he'd been a drinker or a womanizer. But as far as I could tell he was unblemished, until I discovered politics. Then everything collapsed. All that respectability suddenly was gone.

Mother came from a more prosperous family, but as far as the Nazis are concerned she went along with him. She was head counselor in a League of German Girls camp, where everything supposedly was so carefree and beautiful, with everybody helping one another. Only when the synagogues went up in flames things weren't all that beautiful. Then Mother even became a little sad. And long after the war was over I remember her mother talking about how one mustn't intermarry with Jews.

I can't tell you how often I tried over the years to get them to say even a single word of regret. All my father managed was that every regime has its victims. And as to the extermination of the Jews, he once called it a mistake that had done more harm than good.

Later, after I'd left home, I got very interested in Jews. I developed a sort of reverse prejudice. I read everything there was about the concentration camps, about "medical science without humaneness," about the persecutions and exterminations. For a time I identified with the victims. I was so fascinated by every account of survival that I almost felt as though it had happened to me. I had an almost erotic relationship with the victims, and above all the survivors. And then there were the stories about Jews, people who in every respect were the exact opposite of my father—his political naïveté, his compulsive neatness, his moral obtuseness, his intellectual rigidity, his narrowmindedness— traits completely at odds with my preconceptions of Jews.

When I met Alex I promptly told my parents about him. I casually mentioned that I'd met a nice guy, a Jew, and asked them whether they wouldn't like to meet him. Their automatic response was: "But please, no children." When they met him all my mother could say was that he wasn't athletic. That was the most important thing. They did notice that he had brains, but they were afraid of impure children, because those poor little things had such a hard time.

I have an older sister, and my parents didn't have such an easy time with her either. She had a child by a Spaniard, married an American, and at college she dated an African.

At any rate, I continued going with Alex. We now have two children, and I think my parents like him a lot. Still, basically they haven't changed. But Alex helped me rid myself of my tradition. He also refuses to indulge my parents' preconceptions. He questions the things they say, talks to them openly, and he has never shown my kind of acceptance of authority. Many of his traits fascinated me, and others annoyed me. I was a child of nature, liked hiking and the outdoors. When we went on walks I wanted to look at trees, but Alex wasn't particularly interested. He preferred talking. Or when we visited friends who bored him he'd simply get up and leave, something I never would have dared. I was brought up to suffer in silence. In the final analysis

I'm something like a footloose traveler between two camps, the National Socialists and the Jews. I wear a Star of David charm, not that I have gone over to Judaism, but I have a stronger kinship to Judaism than any other faith. We celebrate Hanukkah and Passover with Alex's mother, and I feel very close to her. She accepts me without reservation and without prejudice.

Still there is much that remains strange to me. One of Alex's good friends is a Jew, and when the two of them get together I can hardly understand them. Something goes on between the two of them that I just can't follow. Today I am neither a Carinthian nor a Jew. For a while my relationship with my parents was very strained, but it's gradually improved. I think when they began to realize how deeply attached I was to Alex and that I wasn't going to give him up they relented.

I too went through some changes with regard to Alex. At first everything was strange. For two years I had what might be called the open-mouth syndrome. At first I thought it was due to anti-Jewish prejudices that I had to overcome. Now I know better. These cultural differences do in fact exist, and I try to accept them. Jews *are* different.

My life with Alex undoubtedly has helped me loosen my emotional ties to my parents. Just leaving them physically was not enough. The more important step was removing myself from their ideological sphere. I now have an entirely different attitude toward authority than I used to. I no longer feel that I have to be perfect; I now know it is more important to act instead of waiting for ideal conditions. I am no longer nearly so worried about what others might think. I feel freer and more independent, even though it might seem that being married to a Jew in Austria would be constricting, not liberating. In my case the contrary is true.

The Conciliator

Still, it took a long time before we were ready to marry. Then there came the question of conversion for me, which I didn't want, because I'm not religious. And then of course there was the matter of how the children should be raised. And there, too, we haven't come up with an answer yet. Perhaps it will be up to them to decide which road they'll want to take. Basically it works only when both traditions are kept as far in the background as possible. And so we had a marriage without either priest or rabbi, and the children are not instructed in either the one or the other religion. Whether or not that's a good thing I can't say. Leaving the world of my parents does not necessarily mean becoming completely immersed in Alex's world. Too much there is still strange to me.

When he is together with his Jewish friends I still feel like an outsider. I often get the feeling that an invisible wall has gone up behind which they retreat, leaving me on the outside. Despite all the years I've been with Alex there's still a distance. I've learned to accept it and no longer pretend it doesn't exist. Of course there are times when it's bothered me, but in the final analysis I've been enriched through my life with Alex.

But the tragic part of this expansion of my horizons is that it has meant the loss of my home. And that's what I hold against my parents. I could not go on being a part of the family play they were acting out. But my decision to live with Alex was a decision for isolation. The place I'd grown up in became alien and intolerable. I have hardly any friends; people of my age don't interest me. More and more I have withdrawn into my own little family.

I do, however, think that in our marriage I have given more than Alex. I've become estranged from my parents, but not he from his. Through me he has gotten in touch with this country, with nature, with the landscape, with the beauty of flowers and meadows. What I've gotten is inner turmoil, being torn out of my setting without finding a new one, living with a man who in every respect is the direct opposite of my father. And within the space of a single generation the German nationalist union of a blue-eyed, blond woman and an athletic, slender, Aryan Carinthian youth has produced grandchildren with a foreign, Jewish father. And so perhaps my marriage to Alex is proof of the stupidity and also the transitoriness of ideologies like National Socialism. Perhaps my life here in Austria with a Jew is also my personal contribution to reconciliation and restitution. I couldn't change my parents, but I could get them to accept a Jewish son-in-law. At our wedding they told everybody that they were very happy and that they liked Alex a lot. Fifty years after Auschwitz that must be seen as a step forward, and not such a small one at that.

13

Stefan

The Sufferer

I'M IN the same boat as you. I was the Jew in my family. Father, Mother, Grandmother—all of them conspired to perpetuate the terror in the family. And I was their target. No, they weren't out to kill me, because that would have been too easy. They just wanted to make me suffer, like tearing the wings off a fly and watching it writhe in agony, trying to escape.

I tried to shrug it off, not to let it get me, pretend that it didn't bother me. When something threatened to bother me I wouldn't let my feelings get the upper hand. My parents had a sixth sense for it. They only had to suspect that they had touched a raw nerve and they moved in. They smelled every wound and delighted in finding my weak spot. When I was little I thought the only way I could survive was to hide from them, because all they had to do was see a wound and they'd pour salt into it. If I came home with scraped knees they beat me because I'd dirtied my pants. And if I cried they hit me because I didn't behave like a man. And if I tried to get help they laughed at me. They wore out their shoe leather stepping on me.

There's all that talk about you Jews being the victims of the war. But for those of you who survived, the suffering ended with Hitler's death. But for us, the children of the Nazis, it didn't end. When their world collapsed in ruins and ashes, the heroes of the Third Reich staked out another battleground—the family.

With their invaluable help I developed an inferiority complex of unimaginable dimensions. As a child I was a real idiot, afraid of everything that came my way. In school the other kids beat me up, and it didn't occur to me that I could defend myself. And that's still so. Confronted with authority, I become insecure and tense.

Well, when my first affair broke up I was still stupid enough to confide in my mother, hoping for tenderness and understanding. But all my mother had to say was that I probably had myself to blame. They always did everything in their power to belittle me, regardless of what I asked of them.

Tenderness didn't exist. I can't remember ever being held on my mother's lap or being hugged by her or having my father show any affection. And, of course, no kisses ever.

Later I developed such a confused view of women. In my imagination there existed only two kinds—goddesses and whores. Ninety-nine percent were whores, and the rare goddesses were nowhere to be found. I thought that if I gave them whatever their hearts desired they'd love me. And I did give them whatever I could. I spoiled them, showered them with presents, anticipated all their wishes, but they cheated on me. When I was eighteen I wanted to take my girlfriend—my first one—to Italy, and I saved up for the trip for half a year. I gave her the money for the fare, and that's the last I saw of her. And that was only the beginning.

And then the business of religion. At fourteen I became very religious, going to church regularly, not eating meat on Fridays, and praying all the time. But I soon gave it up when I found that didn't help either. Then I became interested in Buddhism, such a gentle religion, everything is love and touching. It appealed to me. I guess I could have converted, but I was afraid. My parents had robbed me of my willpower. Everything was taboo. I took all they dished out, and it certainly never occurred to me to question them, let alone assert myself.

When I was around twenty I began to feel that nothing was going right, and I started to lose a lot of weight. My whole life was turning into one big setback. I once confided in my father that I wasn't doing so well in the woman department, and all the advice he had to offer was to try a brothel. That's the kind of support I got from him. I think that the only time I was strong was when I was little. But the older I got the weaker I became. Other people as they grow older mature and gradually become independent and able to cope, but I became more insecure and fearful. More and more I looked for protection and security. But who's there now to protect me? Today I'm as endangered as the Jews. That's what I have in common with you. And that's also the reason I find you so sympathetic. I'm sure that in the old days my father brutalized Jews, but after the war there weren't any left. There was only me.

He was proud of what he'd done. He showed them, he used to say. They trembled before him. At first he was in the SA, but he changed over in time. He despised everybody—Jews, Gypsies, homosexuals, Communists—and he still does, except he's too much of a coward to say so out loud. Only behind closed doors, in the safety of his own four walls, does he still dare to play the hero. And after the war I became his chosen victim. I'm not responsible for what my father did. I wasn't born then and have nothing to do with it. And I don't feel responsible for it. And I think that words like "complicity" and "shared responsibility" or "continuing to mourn" are inappropriate. I can't apologize for what my father did. It's he who did it, not I. I have as little to do with what he did as with him. I am an entirely different person, perhaps even his exact opposite. I think of myself as being in the other camp, someone who is suffering under him just as all those others during the Third Reich. Today his brutality and aggressiveness threaten *me*, not those others against whom he keeps on ranting, but that's only talk.

But I've been mistreated by him all my life! Why am I now supposed to feel any special compassion for the victims of National Socialism? For them it's over, and those who survived got lots of assistance. But nobody takes us, the descendants of the Nazis, seriously. On the contrary! Some people even claim that we're just like our fathers. How often did I have to listen to a teacher who saw me fight tell me that that's just what he'd expect of me. Always those allusions to my father.

For a time he was the local SS chief, and the Socialists here really hate him. He sent quite a few of them to prison. None of the Jews returned after the war. Maybe none of them survived, I don't know.

I'm sure I wouldn't have joined the SS if I'd been around then. I would probably have been one of the first to be arrested. I'm not the activist type, not like some of those tough, crude friends of Father's. They can drink beer by the gallon and not get drunk. I get sick after only a glass or two. They can probably

The Sufferer

sleep with any woman, whether they love her or not. They stuff themselves, guzzle and whore their way through life, and anyone who gets in their way is shoved aside, squashed like a pesky fly.

With a father like that I was doomed to fail. There's no escape. I'd trade him for anybody. And my mother isn't any better. She took up where he left off. Of course I made even greater demands on her as regards affection. But she was always one of those upright German women, big and fat, with hands like a butcher. When I was little she'd take my hand as we crossed the street, and when she let go my hand would be white, drained of all blood.

My mother was illegitimate. Her mother worked in her father's grocery. I think my mother never knew who her father was. My grandmother is still alive, a nasty old woman, always in a bad mood, with a beard like a Gypsy.

Grandmother also is still an enthusiastic Nazi. Her favorite saying is that under the next Hitler it won't end like the last time. The next one won't let others bring him down. She's convinced that there'll be another Hitler. And when I try to argue with her or talk of the horrors of the Nazis, she screams at me that I don't know anything about what really happened, that I'd been listening to the propaganda of all the Jews and Communists who are in power today. Once I told her that I was like the Jews, persecuted by the criminals in our society, like the kind she is, and she threw a slipper at me. She can't walk so well anymore.

My father's parents are also still alive. My grandfather was a worker, a mason, and Grandmother stayed at home. My father had two brothers, but both of them died in the war. My father and grandfather can't stand each other. Grandfather always says that my father got out of army service. His brothers at least had fought, against real soldiers. But Father, so he says, made war on defenseless people. But don't misunderstand me, Grandfather was also a confirmed Nazi, except he couldn't stand the SS. He blames them for losing the war. If instead of staying in the hinterland they'd fought at the front, Ivan would be dead today, he says. He hates the Russians, but also the Americans, and of course Jews and blacks. My father's parents live nearby, maybe a half hour's walk from here.

All of them spewed hate and contempt. That's the environment in which I grew up. And it wasn't just politics or views on particular problems. Their attitude encompassed almost all aspects of life. Food, sexuality, and race were permanent fixtures of their catalogue of hatreds. They believe that all those fat cats and whoremongers and everything that isn't German ought to be weeded out.

But isn't sexuality more than that? Doesn't it mean love for another person, the relationship itself, and of course love of nature and of oneself? People like my parents and grandparents can't love anybody or anything. They probably don't even know what it means to love somebody.

I'm entirely different. I think love is the most important thing there is. I also can forgive and even love somebody who has contempt for me. I think that's the most important difference between my parents and me—my ability to feel and give free rein to emotions. My relatives don't know the meaning of sensitivity.

Other than that there's not much to tell about myself. I lived at home until ten years ago, when I graduated from high school. I then moved to Frankfurt to go to college. In school I was always one of the smallest kids and could never assert myself. The other kids used to beat me up, and I was always an outsider, maybe also because I was so pudgy and unathletic. With my dark hair I really looked like a little Jew. And all that macho stuff of the boys also disgusted me. They smoked on the sly, played soccer, and chased girls. I used to go to the playground with them, but I never joined in their games. They let me sit behind the goalpost so that I could chase the ball in case it went past the goalie. One time, I must have been around eleven or twelve, some of the boys went into the bushes with a girl. They pulled down her panties, lifted her skirt, and they all looked. I stood near them and wanted to run away when Gerhard, he was the leader, called me and said I should stick my finger in. I tried to run away, but the others held me and dragged me over to where the girl was. She wasn't scared at all and only laughed. Come on, do it, they all yelled at me and pushed me toward her. I threw myself on the ground and cried and begged them to let me go. They did, but for a long time afterward the boys kept kidding me about it. And what's even worse was that the girls did, too.

I was always alone—at college, too. I lived with an aunt of my mother's, had my own room, but things were no better there than at home. She was just like my parents.

A year ago I met my present girlfriend and moved in with her. She's a little older than I, divorced, and has two children. But she accepts me, isn't aggressive, and for the first time I feel that I can be myself. I'm not doing so well with my studies. All the professors seem to want is rote learning. Comprehension or debate isn't in demand. Here, too, the strong ones take over. It's the same everywhere. One of the professors, by the way, is Jewish, but he is no different either. He was my greatest disappointment. I thought that here's someone I could talk to, who'd understand. But he's so completely assimilated that you couldn't tell that he isn't really one of them. At one of my exams I tried to explain to him that it's not as easy for me as for the others to just sit down and study like an automaton. Do you know what he told me? He said that if thinking poses too great a problem I should go work for a bank. Nice, eh? There's a man whose people were persecuted by the Nazis and almost completely exterminated, and he's learned nothing from that, shows the same sort of authoritarian mentality as my father.

I visit my folks only rarely, at most once a month. Nothing has changed there, always the same speeches and attitudes, the same thing year in, year out. Father abuses the Russians; Mother, the woman who sells vegetables; and neither of them ever asks me anything, except maybe the usual meaningless question about how I'm doing at school. But before I can even answer they're already talking about something else.

Father is retired. After the war he worked for a construction firm as a purchasing agent. His boss was the same sort of Nazi as he. When the two of them got together they talked only about the war and arrests. They both were in the SS and used to arrest people in their apartments, and they're still proud of it. They'd laugh when they told how grown men cried and begged them to let them take some things with them. They were always so proud of their crimes. And these stories didn't upset Mother either. She'd sit there and knit and smile. If I got up and left the room she'd call after me to look at Father, what a hero he was, not a sad sap like me.

Father also shot some people. He said they wanted to run away to avoid military service. He described in detail how he did it. Today he hates the conscientious objectors, but also the officers. The first are nothing but malingerers, and the others sit around in their club and let others do the fighting.

My father's boss, who served with him in the war, also has a

The Sufferer

son. I often used to talk with him about our situation. We're the victims of the Nazis who're still alive, the victims of the survivors. Nobody really understands this. Hitler may have died, but most of his henchmen survived and looked for fresh victims. I now feel drawn to the Gypsies, homosexuals, and Jews. I really feel that I'm one of them. Except for our two cats nobody at home ever showed me any affection. And my father also mistreated the cats. He kicked them and tried to grab them by the tail. Nobody was safe from his brutality.

I can find no allies. I'm also disappointed in the Jews. They wouldn't admit me into their student group, and I have the feeling that they don't want to have anything to do with me. Well, yes, when I think of Israel I can see why. They're no longer the victims. Now the Jews have joined the ranks of the aggressors. Especially the students here are unbelievably supercilious. Solidarity means nothing to them, and they don't see the suffering of others. They can only see themselves and the Holocaust. But that's over and done with. Today others are suffering. The Jews now are better off than anybody else. They're being pampered, just like the blacks.

Only we, the children of the Nazis, are ignored and overlooked. We're the true heirs of the Nazi ideology, the product of the union of the Devil and the tortured creatures of fascism. I no longer feel pity for anybody. All those groups that have sprung up at the university, for South Africa, for Chile, for Soviet Jews. The hell with 'em. They pick their victims as far away as possible so that they don't have to come into contact with them. They demonstrate on behalf of some trees and against rockets only because they're afraid they might be killed. It's all selfishness or pretended compassion to make themselves important. But nobody sees the real victims, the disadvantaged right here at home.

STEFAN

Sensibility and feeling are not in demand in this country. I'm not the victor type and I won't get very far here. Nobody except my new girlfriend knows anything about devotion and sacrifice. I'm a cripple among athletes who talk of nothing but setting records. But they don't even see me, sitting among them in a wheelchair. This world is not my world.

14

Werner

The Mediator

I AM SOMETHING like a connecting link between the guilty and the guiltless, the son of the guilty and the father of the guiltless. I feel obligated to give the guiltless a chance. The guilty had theirs. My generation is the generation of the bad conscience. Perhaps my daughters will one day be proud of me, not only because I'm their father but because I'd been a decent human being, and perhaps they'll even look on me as someone they want to emulate. What a difference between that and my relationship to my father.

But let's get to our story. My father was born in 1902. His parents were North German landowners. Theirs wasn't a big estate, but it did afford them a very good living. My grandfather was killed in World War I, and the manager who took over ran the farm into the ground. My grandmother was then still relatively young. She was only sixteen when my father was born. She moved to Hamburg with the children and remarried. Her second husband was a simple worker. My father, by then in his upper teens, hated him. He was an active Communist and the exact opposite of my father and also of my real grandfather, whose pictures show him on horseback, every inch the landowner. When World War I broke out he volunteered immediately. My grandmother's second husband, on the other hand, was a bookworm, a little sloppy-looking, and you couldn't imagine him riding a horse. My father was very much like his father; he didn't know what to make of his stepfather. During the last war he spent three years in prison as a Communist. But he survived and died in 1975.

I loved him. He was the most important person in my life, next to Grandmother, because it wasn't an accident that she married him after that landowner.

When my grandmother remarried, my father moved away from home. He'd visit his mother only when her husband wasn't at home. My father enlisted in the army in his early youth. The farm was gone, and he wasn't interested in anything else. During the 1930s he joined the SS, I don't know exactly when. There he worked his way up rapidly, was enrolled in the SS cadet training school in Brunswick, and became an officer even though he hadn't taken his college entrance exam.

The two years prior to the outbreak of the war were really my father's best years. He was in the thick of things—at the smashing of the SA, the waves of arrests, the anti-Jewish campaigns. Still he wasn't the sort of monster you might think. When the war broke out he operated behind the front, in the occupied territories, on the Eastern front. He periodically came back to

The Mediator

Hamburg, always for a few days, visited his mother, and then was gone again.

I've become convinced beyond a doubt that he was transferred to Auschwitz in mid-1944, a promotion of sorts, a special assignment. He stayed there exactly one day and then volunteered for the front. Maybe his refusal to speak dates back to that time. He was wounded in early 1945 and returned home at the end of the war minus one leg.

I was born in 1946. My mother is fifteen years younger than my father. She met my father toward the end of the war in an army hospital. They married when the war ended and have lived in Hamburg ever since.

Because my father had volunteered for front-line service at the last moment he wasn't investigated or prosecuted after the war. He became a civil servant; they waived the university entrance exam requirement. And even though he was an invalid, he advanced in his job and reached a fairly high level. My mother stayed at home.

My father was a strange man, the most taciturn person I've ever known. It must have been the war and his experiences before his active front-line service that made him that way. That was his real handicap. There were crutches for his legs, but there were none for his silence. He had powerful arms and was very agile, and he used to go on long walks. But that silence of his was terrible.

If it hadn't been for my mother he might have committed suicide. She is such a blend of German sternness and Slavic warmth, tall and rangy, with perpetually damp hands which she keeps wiping on her apron. Actually, she had two children, my father and me—the one small with two legs, and the other grown up with only one leg. Mother ignored my father's silences; she talked incessantly. She'd ask a question and promptly answer it herself. I think Father liked it. He'd sit next to her quietly, nod every now and then, and look relaxed, unlike his usual tense and nervous manner, particularly when I talked to him.

I grew up in Hamburg, attended school there, and also the university. But the most influential person during my childhood was my grandfather. Even though he wasn't my real grandfather, still that's what I called him. He was always in a good mood, despite the three years in a Nazi prison. He used to wear a beret, even indoors. And he was never without his pipe, which he chewed on when it went out. He was a hippie and a dropout long before the sixties.

He and my grandmother lived near us, a few minutes by bike, in a tiny apartment in the rear of an old building—kitchen, living room, and bedroom. The living room was unbelievable. Books and newspapers were piled up everywhere, on every chair, on the floor, on every available surface. If I wanted to sit down, Grandpa tilted the chair forward so that everything slid down, pushed the papers away with his foot, and offered me the chair. A big dining table covered by a heavy rug instead of a tablecloth stood in the center of the room. Overflowing bookshelves lined the walls. And in the midst of all this sat Grandpa at the table. In front of him a pile of newspapers, pipe in mouth, elbows propped on the table. That's why he liked the rug so much.

Grandma sat either in the kitchen or in an easy chair in the living room, an old, worn-out chair which at one time may have been green, but now the covering was threadbare and had badly mended tears. And Grandma sat there, smoking and knitting. She always knitted, but I never saw her finish a sweater or socks.

Since both of them smoked, the air in the apartment was vile. The first thing I did when I came in was to open the windows. And then Grandpa would pound the table and say, "Yes, yes, our Werner, he wants us to live forever."

These two old people were my real home. I went there every day after school. First I went to my house to eat, because Grandma was a terrible cook, got rid of my book bag, and immediately rushed off to Grandpa. He'd already read all the morning papers and clipped the things he wanted to discuss with me.

His comments on the important events of the day went something like this: "Just look at this idiot, you can see how stupid he looks. And just listen to all that nonsense of his." And while he was talking he'd hold the clipping in his hand, and with his free hand bang on the table, laughing all the while. He amused himself by ridiculing these types. He talked to me man to man. I never had the feeling of being just a child. Grandpa discussed important matters with me, and I was proud.

Afterward Grandma would bring in cookies and coffee for both of us. It would never have occurred to her to give me hot chocolate instead of coffee.

Of course Grandpa influenced my politics. All the things that Father should have told me I learned from Grandpa, and naturally the conversation often turned to the Nazis, usually with very dramatic gestures and no theoretical discourses. He did it in his typical fashion, pointing to a picture of somebody in the paper with these words: "Look, Werner. That's how somebody looks who's murdered thousands of people. No! Not with his own hands. Heaven forbid! After all, he's no monster. He was a high official and signed documents and handed them to somebody. These others then read them, and because they were drawn in such simple, clear language they understood them. And then these people ordered others to murder still others. That's how simple it all was. Everyone had his special assignment."

He used to tell me about life in prison, about the tortures and the daily executions. In the three years he spent there he met thirty-seven other prisoners. Of these, twenty-four were executed.

The older I got the more questions I asked. I didn't just sit there quietly and listen to him. And naturally we once also talked about my father. I knew that the two were not on good terms and that my father visited his mother only when Grandpa wasn't around. But that was more my father's doing. Never once did I hear Grandpa say one word of criticism about my father. On the contrary. He usually said that my father was one of the few who realized in time that he had gotten involved with criminals, and that was laudable, but that it had destroyed him and that today he's a broken man.

Everything that I know about my father I learned from Grandpa—his early enthusiasm, his fanatical allegiance to the Nazis, and his hatred and contempt of Grandpa.

When I was fourteen something crucial happened. I was sitting with Grandpa reading the papers, and as usual he went on about this idiot and that criminal and the dangerous stupidity of still another one—his usual commentary on politicians. And once again we began to talk about my father. Grandpa was trying to explain the role of the SS to me when Grandma came in with our coffee. She set the cups on the table, spilling some of the coffee with her trembling hands, and some of the cookies also slid off the plate. But this time she didn't go back to her easy chair but kept on standing in front of us, waiting. Grandpa said nothing and kept on stirring his coffee.

"Go on," she said. Grandpa said nothing. "You can't keep the truth from him forever." Grandpa stuffed a handful of cookies into his mouth and gulped his coffee.

"If you won't tell him, I will," Grandma persisted, still standing. Grandpa went on eating his cookies.

"It was your father," she said. "He denounced Grandpa. That's why he had to spend three years in prison."

I didn't understand anything, didn't know who denounced whom and why, and why Grandpa therefore had to go to prison. I probably knew more about the Nazis than most others my age. Still I didn't understand what this was supposed to mean.

It turned into a long afternoon. I didn't get home until late. Grandpa told me that during the war he'd worked in a munitions plant, and there he became part of a resistance group made up of Communists, Socialists, and some Catholics. They tried to sabotage production, but their most important job was to pass on information about arms shipments to the Allies via secret channels. Grandpa called his role in the group small potatoes. He distributed leaflets, painted anti-Nazi slogans on walls at night, and occasionally delivered letters whose contents he didn't know. Once he hid a comrade the SS was looking for. But the big things, he told me, he found out only after they were over.

Once my father returned home on leave and visited his mother when Grandpa wasn't home and came upon an anti-Nazi leaflet. Grandpa was always very careless and left things lying about. It's a miracle that his carelessness hadn't gotten him in trouble sooner. At any rate, my father didn't say anything while he was in the apartment, but the very next day Grandpa was arrested. Only much later, long after the war was over, did he confess to his mother that he was the one who'd denounced Grandpa.

Grandpa was very composed when he told me the whole story. There was no hatred, no reproach, no bitterness. Grandma was much more excited. She kept on interrupting, saying, "My own son, can you imagine such a thing." Then the two of them almost got into a fight. It was the first time I saw them arguing. But Grandpa found excuses for my father. He tried to explain to me how things were at the time and the situation my father was in. He wouldn't listen to criticism about him.

I was devastated and said nothing. Somehow I couldn't understand it all. Someone denounces somebody else, and they all belong to the same family. On that day I found it difficult to look Grandpa in the eye, as though I too was responsible for what my father had done, sitting there in his place, filled with shame and a bad conscience. All I wanted to do was go home and confront my father and ask him: "How could you do this to me? Yes, to me. From now on I can no longer feel free and uninhibited with Grandpa."

For the first time the story of my father was more than just a story. I suddenly became aware of the possibility that my father's deed could also be part of me, even though I wasn't even born at the time. This feeling guilty for something one hadn't done oneself yet which also hadn't been done by just anybody but by one's own father hit me unexpectedly and took me by surprise.

Much later I also drew another lesson from this situation. Of course I'd also known before what had happened under the Nazis and that denunciations within families were not unheard of. But until this time these were only stories, things that had happened in other places to other people. Only the involvement of my father and Grandpa made it personal. There no longer was a way out, no escape into the stories of others, no shaking of the head over the barbarity of strangers. My own father had suddenly become one of them.

I tell my classes about this episode as an example of how the personal fate of a person close to you can turn theoretical explanations into reality. It brought me awareness of the triteness of fascism, of the cruelty and also the banality of everyday life with Nazis and Communists in one and the same family.

What sort of a family was this? A man denounces his stepfather, the husband of his own mother, knowing that he might be passing a death sentence, a man who is so fanatical a Nazi that he denounces his own family. After that he's assigned to a concentration camp as an officer, perhaps even as a reward for his betrayal, and after only a day he volunteers for the front, where he loses a leg and survives only through a stroke of luck.

When I finally confronted my father with what I'd learned, he looked at me with his tired eyes, got up, and left the room. And I never again brought up the subject. My father wasn't able to talk about it at all. A speechless figure. He'd say a few words about the weather, about food, but when the conversation turned to politics he stopped talking, as did Mother, who otherwise was such a great talker. A wall went up which I couldn't break through, and probably also didn't want to. In some way I understood that I wouldn't get very far. The two of them apparently had agreed not to talk about certain matters. And even if I approached my mother when Father wasn't at home, the only thing she'd say was: "There's no use, Werner. Leave us alone. And if you try to force him, he'll grow even more silent."

And so I let it lie. I finished high school and went on to study sociology and political science. Of course the education I'd gotten through Grandpa proved valuable, and the student uprisings of the sixties came as no surprise. I joined the Trotskyists, demonstrated, distributed leaflets, contributed political articles to obscure magazines, and was determined to bring about the historic union between workers and revolutionary students. Unfortunately the oppressed masses we wanted to liberate weren't interested and beat us up when we came to their plants.

I was still living with my parents. They never criticized me. I visited my grandfather as often as time permitted. He wasn't all that enthusiastic about my political engagement and said I should finish my studies before making revolution. The other way around wasn't quite so good.

Grandpa grew old and feeble. He had difficulty reading and waited for me to come and read the papers to him. But the fact that he couldn't read himself didn't stop him from commenting.

Grandpa died in 1975. He was almost ninety. And a few months after that Grandma also died. And in 1976 my father died. Within the space of a year I lost all my relatives except my mother. She's still alive.

I finished my studies, married Ulrike, and got a teaching position at the university at Frankfurt, where we live with our two daughters.

I devote all my energy to teaching. Seminars on fascism, lectures about the resistance movement, excursions to concentration camps, and so on. I try everything. And even the shift to the right in recent years has not deterred me. Here at the university we can tell that the wind has shifted. Nobody hampers us and nobody interferes with our curriculum, but when it comes to the funding of research programs it becomes clear which projects are considered worthwhile and which aren't. What bothers me most is the tendency to put Nazis and Communists in the same boat. In the discussions with students I can see how widespread this view has become. They even justify the murder of the Communists. I've often heard this in my seminars. The majority of today's twenty-year-olds certainly aren't right-wingers, and most definitely not neo-Nazis. But they are skeptical about the resistance movement. Resistance to the state seems somehow dirty, unclean, something decent people oughtn't to do. It almost looks as though the young people today feared that someday they might have to defend themselves. Some students once even lodged a complaint against me. They didn't want to be taught by a Communist; that wasn't sufficiently objective for them. In answer to the question why they thought I was a Communist they said that I keep on stressing the role of the Communists in the anti-Nazi resistance. This historic fact was more than they were willing to accept. And it made no difference that in that very seminar we'd discussed the executed resistance fighters, namely those murdered by the Stalinists in the 1950s.

But there are also others, those who want to know everything, who come to me after class and ask me to recommend books and who are determined to bury the past. They give me hope. They remind me of my role as a connecting link. And I was privileged to grow up among survivors, and that privilege obliges me to hand on everything I know.

In retrospect I of course know that I am the child of an SS officer, that I come from a family that played a direct role in the greatest crime in human history. My father's leaving the SS and his voluntary front-line service came very late and in my opinion doesn't offset the things he'd done before. The denunciation of a member of his family still troubles me when I think of him.

But in a way the varied fate of my family also typifies twentieth-century Germany. One grandfather is killed in World War I, the other one becomes a Communist, the father becomes an SS officer and denounces his stepfather, the son sees the Communist grandfather as his model and becomes a left-winger —an improbable, checkered history.

And then the women: a grandmother who led two diametrically opposed lives, going from a landowner and a twenty-room house with maids and cooks and nursemaids to a leftist worker in a three-room apartment, and a mother of unimaginable gentleness living with a desperate husband.

Grandpa, who incidentally had never been a Stalinist and had no use for the Eastern bloc bureaucrats, has remained my example and my positive German model. And I stress "German." I was spared the fate of many of my generation of having hate drive a wedge between me and the older generation. I loved that old man, and he remains a symbol for me, proof that that "other" Germany has always existed as well.

Postscript

The Misfortune of Being Born Too Late

I<small>N</small> FEBRUARY 1987 portions of this book were serialized in three consecutive issues of the German news magazine *Der Spiegel*. Initially the editors had some misgivings about running the series, wondering whether their magazine was the appropriate forum for treating this theme in this form, and also whether reminiscences about the Third Reich and its aftermath hadn't reached the saturation point. However, the response to the publication exceeded all expectations. The phones never stopped ringing in the editor's office, nor in the office of the book's publisher or in my home. The calls came from all over the world, from journalists, from people who identified with some of the persons interviewed, from numerous ordinary readers who found these stories compelling.

After the appearance of the last installment, *Der Spiegel* published a selection of the letters that had poured in, among them one by a teacher who was born in 1940, the son of an SS officer who was sentenced to death and executed. This now forty-seven-year-old man addressed his letter to the nineteen-year-old Stefanie:

Dear Stefanie,

I was born in 1940, the son of an *Oberregierungsrat* [chief administrative officer] and *SS-Obersturmbannführer* who was executed in 1948 for his Nazi crimes. I'm a teacher (though to listen to my students not a typical one) of math, science, economics, and history.

You ask who knows whether things were really so bad back then.

Believe me: they were worse. I have original death lists of prisoners exterminated in a labor camp in Brunswick. My father signed many death warrants. His depositions on these "violations" are in my possession.

You ask how about all the happy faces on the photos.

Well, what kind of photos were taken and made public and what kind weren't? Who took the pictures? Who and which photos were considered "harmful, demoralizing, inciting," and more such insane nonsense?

To judge by the elections, about half of our nation welcomed Hitler. You ask why.

Well, many had really been having a bad time of it for too long, and then there were those who could gain power, success, and importance only in such a system.

The Misfortune of Being Born Too Late

My father, for example, with his low score on his law exam. That took care of his ever becoming a juvenile judge. So he went into the party, and through it into government service, and on to the criminal police, to the Gestapo, and ultimately to the SS (automatic), and a rapid rise to high position.

Other "victors," doctors and professors, got rid of the Jewish competition (and with that many a clinic deteriorated). And all those street fighters, all those bums and drinking buddies, who didn't want to or couldn't learn. They were suddenly wanted, were allowed to harass intellectuals. That was something! What a feeling! And the military! For years they had had to hide because the others had won. Now they were needed.

Just imagine if a campaign were launched today to "toughen up" all those softies, crybabies, and religious types by forcing them to work. Wouldn't you want to participate— as an "expert," so to speak—for the cause, good pay, and acceptance? You could forget about not having finished school and being unemployed! Well? Be honest. There you are.

Do you have any idea how many fancy stores in Düsseldorf were "bought" from enemies of the regime and Jews for ridiculous sums? Today these are the fat cats who mistreat their employees, "bend" the laws and cheat on taxes, and don't give you a job because you don't know how to cringe.

You ask should we Germans continue to cringe?

No, and I don't do it, and your sweater-wearing teacher is an idiot. We should mourn occasionally, and we shouldn't have any illusions, and shouldn't blame everything on past "evils." For that's not what matters. What matters are all the petty meannesses and corruptions.

And that's true for everyone! Also for the French and the Eskimos.

You'd like to belong to the "victors." With your background that's very understandable. But what's a victor? Every victor has his vanquisher. After the Six-Day War in Israel I saw victors by the dozen. Disgusting. They thought they could do anything to anybody. (The really brave ones, on the other hand, were shaken and very quiet!)

And now to the "great" looks. Uniforms do a lot for self-esteem. But the only ones afraid of them are those who are scared shitless anyway.

So one makes a negative choice if one hopes to impress with bravado and guts. Smart people know that the guy in the uniform needs it, just like the guy who's impotent needs his Porsche.

My old man also looked fantastic, especially because his cap covered his incipient bald spot. He died standing tall and brave.

Has it occurred to you that maybe you and your friends are making things too easy for yourselves with your contempt and spite, and maybe that that's not enough in the long run?

> With affection, Dirk Kuhl,
> Remscheid (Northrhine-Westphalia)

I received a similar letter with the request to forward it to Stefanie.

Also shortly after the publication of the book, there appeared an article by the well-known Swiss writer Adolf Muschg in the *Frankfurter Rundschau*, a liberal Frankfurt daily. He called his essay "The Misfortune of Being Born Too Late," an allusion to

The Misfortune of Being Born Too Late

something Chancellor Helmut Kohl had said on a visit to Israel. Kohl had spoken of the "good fortune of being born too late," meaning that because of his age he was spared involvement in the crimes of the Nazis. Kohl's formulation came to symbolize a feeling of innocence in Germany, and various political groupings and political scientists employed it in trying to define the newly developing sense of German self-worth.

But Adolf Muschg's intention was to examine the education of these new Germans, and he used the interview with the nineteen-year-old Stefanie as his starting point, above all her account of what happened in her school, how her teacher reacted to the provocative question whether things had really been so bad in the Third Reich.

Muschg posed an interesting question, namely, whether the teachers weren't using the horrors of the Nazi era as a club against the children. The teachers, born during the war or shortly thereafter, pose as the messengers of the horrors, and they do so in a way that denies that they themselves may share in the responsibility. They claim to be the good people, the decent ones. Some of them even identify with the persecuted of the Nazi era, only because they are now in opposition to the government. Or they contend that those who disagree with them on issues like atomic energy, disarmament, or environmental pollution display a quasi-fascist political mentality. This leads to the inevitable conclusion that those who today think differently would also have been among the persecuted "back then." Divergence in political opinion in Germany today can thus be subsumed in the categories of "victim" and "perpetrator."

Many teachers see themselves as belonging to this category of potential "victims." They therefore present the history of the Nazi era as a potential threat to them here and now. In this scenario the students become possible "perpetrators" if they are not ready to condemn what they are shown in the documentaries. And so these teachers conclude that they themselves can never be counted among the perpetrators, whereas the students may.

And Adolf Muschg concluded: "The teacher wants the students to freeze before the authority of Auschwitz, but what they feel instead is that they are being deprived of their freedom of movement."

The students feel that they have the same right as the teacher to consider themselves as part of a generation that did not participate. And more and more they defend themselves, often instinctively, against the schools' use of the Nazi crimes just to put pressure on them. They tend to react with a blatant display of callousness, indifference, and sympathy with the perpetrators. Their objective is provocation, not neo-Nazism.

An editor of *Der Spiegel* showed the interview with Stefanie to his eighteen-year-old son. He was astonished by the boy's reaction. About half of his class, he said, would react the same. In Germany, the response to the book focused overwhelmingly on the interview with Stefanie. In countless forums and discussions forty- and fifty-year-old men and women asked what they had done wrong, how it was possible for young people to arrive at so uncritical a stance on the Nazi era, particularly since today's teachers and pedagogues consider themselves dyed-in-the-wool antifascists. A majority of the teachers were themselves students during the turbulent 1960s and were influenced by the student movement, and they are convinced not only that they are different but also that they teach differently.

In the discussions the question was raised whether it makes any sense to continue to show the youngsters films about the

The Misfortune of Being Born Too Late

Nazi crimes, to urge them to read about it, and to take them on tours of concentration camps—indeed, whether it is right to reduce the history of the Third Reich simply to one of the murder and slaughter of innocent people. One ought to have the courage, it was suggested by some, to talk as well about the enthusiasm, about all those to whom the end of the war meant not liberation but defeat.

In the forty years since the war ended, the problems facing the pedagogues have changed radically. While those who came of age during that time complain that when they were young they were told next to nothing about the Nazi era, today's youth complain that all they hear is that they were, and perhaps still are, a nation of murderers and accomplices.

A passage of the book on this very problem, something Anna said, is often mentioned in this context:

> Of course I knew that there had been concentration camps and that 6 million Jews had been murdered. We'd been told about it in school. But I had also been told fairy tales in school, stories like Little Red Riding Hood. And we learned about the Crusades and later, when I was older, about the French Revolution. And still later, about World War II and the gas chambers. But who, for God's sake, had ever told us that our own parents had been there?

The two generations of teachers and pedagogues that have been active in the schools since the end of the war reject all complicity and guilt. The first ignored this chapter of Germany's history because they grew up during the Nazi reign, and they reduced these years to a compilation of dates and battles, and the second presented the horrors of the war as proof of the guilt of

165

others and of their own innocence. But this ignored the fear and uncertainty that one's own father or mother may possibly have played an active role in the crimes of the Nazis. The postwar Germans could not expect help from any quarter. The parents either remained silent or did not tell the truth. The teachers either minimized what had happened or roundly blamed all who were living then. And the official agencies, with their wonted objectivity and detachment, proclaimed that the investigation of the history of one's own family posed almost insuperable problems.

Shortly after the publication of the book I received numerous, almost identically worded letters. In sparse sentences the writers told of the history of their parents—of fathers who died some time ago, that all they knew about them was that they'd been in the SS, that they'd never questioned them, but that they now were curious about what their fathers had actually done. They wanted to know whether Germany had archives or a documentation center where they could find out more about their fathers. Many were consumed by the fear that their fathers might not have been the ordinary soldiers they'd always claimed to have been. For many of them the link between the terrible pictures of that time and the possible direct participation of their fathers is a source of acute anxiety. Naturally what they hope to learn is that their fathers hadn't done anything; still, they want to know the truth.

Of course others also were heard from. *Der Spiegel* published letters heaping abuse on both the publisher and myself. Then there were the usual anonymous letters and telephone calls, often in the middle of the night. But the negative responses were comparatively few, almost minuscule. The same holds true for critical reviews. A small daily paper in Salzburg, Austria, rejected the book with the argument that it indicts the innocent children of those who have no share in the collective guilt.

Nonetheless, this does not mean that the general reaction in Germany and Austria was overwhelmingly positive. Most of the reviewers seemed too apprehensive or too careful to reveal their true feelings. There is a reaction of silence, and it is an interesting one. Even though Austrians were disproportionately well represented in the SS command of concentration camps and other centers of extermination, the reaction to the book in Austria can be summed up in one word: silence. Whereas the interest in the book, above all in Europe, was great—it is being translated into almost every European language—Austrian journalists ignored it. Except for the previously cited negative review in Salzburg, no paper or TV or radio station has mentioned it. The repressive mechanism continues to operate effectively in Austria to this day. In Germany I couldn't keep up with all the requests for lectures and discussions, but only two such events were planned in Austria. They took place in Graz; the first drew a crowd of twenty people at most. The second, scheduled for that same afternoon for students in a youth center, drew an audience of ten, and even they seemed to be there by accident. I later learned that the schools had not bothered to publicize it.

The same mentality that underlies the Waldheim affair is at work here: we weren't the ones and it's not our problem. It is a strange feeling indeed to be living in a country and writing about its history—and about the effects of that history on contemporary problems and on the "new" Austrians—and to be boycotted and ignored by all the political camps and groups.

In Germany the reaction was altogether different. In numerous meetings I had the opportunity to talk with representatives of both the older and younger generations. Many of them were brave enough to talk about their parents, their conflicts with them, and what it means to live with the fear of perhaps being the child of a murderer. The title of the book gave rise to lively discussion. The postwar generation of Germany is trying to come to terms with the questions of guilt and responsibility. For decades their parents had told them that they did not feel responsible for what had happened, but they themselves, the children of the "innocent," often reacted altogether differently. *Der Spiegel* published a letter from Georg Kopp, a nineteen-year-old man living in Brunswick, in which he states: "As the child of fascist grandparents I feel guilty, guilty that even after forty years of post-Nazi rule National Socialist ideology is still so widespread."

Others accused me of failing to give the new Germans a chance, of holding them responsible for the deeds of their parents. I tried to convince my critics that the title was not my idea but rather that of the interviewees themselves. It was not I who tried to impose guilt on that generation; it was they who *felt* guilty. And the intensity and fervor of those who insisted that they did not feel responsible underscore how heavily the problem of guilt weighed on them. Whether their reaction took the form of acceptance or defensiveness, the issue of their parents' possible involvement in the crimes of the Nazis was a crucial factor in the postwar generation's search for a new identity.

The education of the parents before and during the Nazi era and their attitudes toward authority and obedience help explain the profound difference between them and the postwar generation. In order to understand these forty-year-olds and their children, let us recall the words of those who educated their parents:

This youth [Hitler said in 1938] is taught nothing but to

think German, act German, and when these boys of ten
enter our organization, then four years later they move on
to the Hitler Youth, and there we keep them for another
four years; we certainly don't turn them over to our old
class and caste despoilers but take them into the party
immediately, into the Labor Front, into the SA or SS, into
the National Socialist Motor Corps, and so forth . . . and
they don't get away from us for the rest of their lives.

And this is what the Führer had to say about his approach to
the education of German youth:

My pedagogy is harsh. Weakness must be chipped away.
The youth that will grow up in my fortresses will frighten
the world. I want a brutal, authoritarian, fearless, cruel
youth. Youth must be all of this. It must be able to bear
pain. It must not have anything weak and gentle. The light
of the free, marvelous beast of prey must once again shine
from their eyes. I want my youth to be strong and beautiful.
. . . Then I will be able to create the new.

The children of the perpetrators have parents who grew up
under these guidelines, or if already grown up, were told to
educate their children accordingly. Moreover, the end of the
war did not mean salvation or liberation for that generation. In a
book of extracts from diaries between the years 1938 and 1945
(published in the Federal Republic in 1984), we find that regardless of age or position, they experienced the end of the war
as a catastrophe, not as a liberation. For the Germans, whether
they were children or soldiers or older, a world had collapsed.
The new teachers in the schools may have accepted the new

curricula, but *they* did not change their allegiance. In the safety of their own homes they continued to celebrate the ideals of the Nazi era, or at least refused to reject them or to acknowledge errors.

On the whole, the descendants of the perpetrators and their fellow travelers could not make a positive identification with their parents. During my many discussions in Germany, men and women again and again talked of the problem they had accepting their parents as models. The only way they could do so was to accept them as they were, without questioning them or doubting them. Another alternative was to wait for the age factor to come into play. Many said that the death of their parents finally brought them the longed-for liberation. Once they no longer felt they had to protect their parents and make excuses for them, they were able to break away from them without having to face up to them directly. Denying the existence of problems invariably went hand-in-hand with a detachment and defensiveness that made life and contact with their parents possible.

A forty-year-old man, a doctor by profession, wrote to me that he struggled all his life to break with his parents but never managed to. As a young man he found out by accident that his father had been an SS officer directly involved in Nazi crimes. He tried to question him about it but desisted when his father reacted very aggressively and denied all guilt. He wrestled with the problem of whether to break with his parents or simply to ignore it. He decided on the latter course. In his letter he told me that he just wasn't able to break with his parents and never see them again. His father died two years ago and now his relationship with his mother is much better and more honest as well. Now both of them often talk about his father, and his mother also talks about the war more readily.

The Misfortune of Being Born Too Late

Other communications I have received testify to the enormous influence of parental behavior on their children's efforts to develop a feeling of self-worth. In order to develop pride, these new Germans have had to reject their parents, breaking with them completely. The only other alternative open to them was to follow in their parents' footsteps. Either decision is made with misgivings. The one seems unfair because it means standing up to one's parents, and the other excuses or even sanctions parental misdeeds.

Another reaction may be described as "disappointment over irreconcilability." Many complain that their hope for reconciliation is not respected or accepted by the victims and their descendants. So much has been done since the end of the war, they say, and still it is not enough. What more can they do to finally make peace? Even those who condemn the crimes of the Nazis and take an unambiguous stand on the attitude of their parents are bitter because they are still met with rejection. They cannot understand that reconciliation can only be a reaching out, and it is the prerogative of the victim either to accept or reject it. They feel rejected and are hurt when their outstretched hand is not immediately taken in gratitude. One review in a German paper included this passage: "For years we have supported Israel, have tried to make financial restitution, thousands of tourists visit the country of the Jews, but everything seems to be in vain. We Germans are still treated as if nothing has changed."

From these arguments it appears that the Germans expect an end to expiation and repentance. The yearning for a sort of "zero hour," for an unencumbered rapprochement, frequently leads to irritation that these expectations are not met. A young German at one of our meetings said that she is tired of always being asked about the Nazis when she travels. She wasn't around then and detests what the Nazis did, but she, a young German, feels that she is being treated unfairly when she is constantly taxed with that chapter of German history. These discussions have been known to culminate in a new anti-Semitism, in which references to "Jewish vengefulness" are heard, frequently in combination with critical comments about present-day Israel, its policy in Lebanon, and the conduct of Jews in South Africa.

Comparisons are drawn between the Jews in Israel today and the Germans back then. They say that we can now see that Jews can also behave aggressively and unfairly, and they don't always see themselves as perpetrators vis-à-vis the victims. Many young Germans feel frustrated, they say, because whatever they do isn't enough and it is all useless.

An interesting question touched on by a number of reviewers was how I, a Jew, came to write this book. Some Jews have maintained that this is a topic that would be better left to a descendant of a Nazi family. Others, on the other hand, believe that only a Jew could write about it, and that the interviewees certainly would have responded differently to someone else. Some have been struck by the fact that it has taken so many years for a book like this to be written, and by a Jew to boot. In the meantime a third generation has almost reached adulthood, and some who were born after the war are now grandparents. But it is part of the repressive process of the postwar era that up to now nothing has been written about the children of the perpetrators. And so it is no accident that I, a Jew, someone not burdened by past guilt, should have tackled the question of how these descendants of the perpetrators come to terms with the problem. In some of the discussions I was asked whether I hadn't attacked some of my subjects rather aggressively and thereby hampered an objective view of their attitudes.

The Misfortune of Being Born Too Late

Of course it wasn't a "normal situation" for the interviewees, nor for me as a Jew to be talking with the children of Nazis. But the problems of distortion or of truthfulness or openness never arose. Many with similar histories told me that in all these years they could not get themselves to confide in anyone who shared their background but that they could imagine doing so with someone altogether different. And the assertion that a Jew should not concern himself with these questions was roundly rejected. Just as Jews cannot be the only ones to write about Jews, one cannot expect Nazis or the children of Nazis to be the only ones to write about themselves.

Both my books of interviews, with the children of the perpetrators and the children of the victims, brought on a generational conflict. The older generation does not want to hear or read about their past; but the second generation is gradually beginning to investigate and absorb the influence of that era into their own lives. Recently, the grandson of the Austrian Nazi leader Seyss-Inquart, the former Reich Commissar for the Netherlands, offered the Jewish museum in Amsterdam his financial and personal support for an exhibition. His offer gave rise to heated debate. It was rejected, but after a wave of demonstrations in support of young Seyss-Inquart, the sponsors reconsidered and decided that this young man's gesture might possibly make a valuable contribution to a renewal—perhaps a more important one than many a financial contribution.

A new generation is trying to put the problems of guilt, complicity, and responsibility behind them. In the new climate of openness we hear expressions of both perplexity and indifference. Consideration of the parents and grandparents perhaps is no longer as crucial as ten or twenty years ago. For those between the ages of twenty and forty, the history of the Third

Reich is not a living presence. The last rubble heaps have been cleared away, the old Nazis are either in retirement or dead. High public office is now held by people who were then either still unborn or very young. The "old ones" are bewildered by the open rejection of and curiosity about the past of these "young ones."

In trying to sum up the German reaction to this book I would have to say that doubt is the dominant factor: doubt whether they, the new Germans, are really so different from their parents and grandparents, whether a residue of the perpetrator mentality is not part of their psychological baggage. That doubt holds enormous hope. Until now the people in Germany were convinced that what happened in the past could never happen again. That is no longer true today. Now they say that they want to see the threat in time and defend themselves against it. They say that anything is possible and that therefore they have to be vigilant. And this vigilance is a greater safeguard against a possible fascist resurgence in Germany than the conviction that it cannot happen again.

But Germany is not the only country in which this book has stirred up a debate about the past. Thus in Holland, for instance, the publisher plans to append a chapter dealing with the children of Dutch Nazis. The French edition will carry an introduction discussing the role of French collaborators, at a time when the trial of Klaus Barbie is in the news. The Greek-language edition makes reference to its former military dictatorship.

Thus these interviews with the children of German and Austrian Nazis have led to an examination of the past in other European countries, and the effects of the deeds of the parents on their children counteract the efforts of those who would

The Misfortune of Being Born Too Late

rather let things slide into a memory hole. Today, fifty years after the Kristallnacht, the history of the Nazi era is more alive than ever. Perhaps Hans Frank ("The Slaughterer of Poles," the Nazi governor of Poland, who was implicated in the murder of millions) wasn't all that wrong when he said in one of his interrogations that "a thousand years will pass and they will not take away this guilt of Germany." (However, in his final words he retracted this statement.)

Still, there is no denying that the years separating us from the Third Reich grow longer. A third generation stands on the threshold of adulthood, and some who are children now are the great-grandchildren of the perpetrators. The last surviving activists of that era are at least sixty-five years old, and very few of the most culpable are still alive. More and more, the Nazi terror is becoming part of history, like World War I. And it is also becoming more and more improbable that the experiences and personal histories of the perpetrators and their henchmen will be handed on within the families.

That is what makes the response to this book in and outside of Germany so astonishing. It demonstrates that despite the years that have passed since the Nazis came to power in 1933, and since their defeat in 1945, interest in that era by the successor generation has not abated. "How could it have happened?" is a question that continues to be asked by the grandchildren of the Nazis. The hope of so many old activists—that time will bring forgetfulness and that Germans will be accepted by the democratic world without being reminded of their dark past—has been disappointed. There can be no new Germany without the remembrance of its history. There can be no new German democrats if they do not accept the National Socialist era as part of their own history.

I came away from these interviews convinced that the next generation will also grow up burdened by the knowledge that their forebears were involved in the greatest mass murder in history, or at the very least had done nothing to stop it. And those who are convinced that their fathers or mothers or grandparents or even great-grandparents were implicated in the murder of innocent people will have to live with it. It will not get easier for them, for it seems that time does not heal these wounds. On the contrary: a new generation has achieved positions of eminence throughout the world and refuses to accept the proposition that those crimes, committed before they were born, should therefore be forgotten. The fact that Nazi war criminals are being extradited from the United States to the Soviet Union, the fact that the concern about the possible involvement in a Nazi crime can induce a friendly country to bar a head of state, are indicative of this attitude. True, more and more members of the younger generation say that none of this is their business and that they do not feel responsible for the acts of their grandparents. But even in these cases the frequently desperate defensiveness bespeaks a feeling of guilt or shame about something that concerns them but in which they had no part and shows the effect of the past on the next generation.

Both reactions, defensiveness and acceptance, indicate that young Germans are indeed preoccupied with the past. Indifference is rare.

These talks with the children of the Nazis helped me to understand them better. I now know why they never talked about their parents and their role during the war. They knew so

The Misfortune of Being Born Too Late

little about it. I now understand that it must be terrible to grow up not knowing whether one's father was a direct participant in a crime, that it is possible to be afraid of questioning him and finding out what happened. I can also understand that many do not want to burden their parents with recriminations. Their parents are old and feeble and no longer able to defend themselves. I can imagine all of that without, however, feeling pity. I can imagine how difficult it must be to have a Nazi for a father, but I cannot imagine defending him. I can imagine that it is not easy to grow up with a mother who keeps on defending the father and seeks to prevent a clash between the child and the father, but I cannot understand applauding her. I now understand that it takes an enormous amount of strength and self-assurance to criticize one's parents, to question them, let alone to break with them.

Yet I have no understanding for someone who does not do it. I do not reproach those who defend their parents, and in extreme instances even admire them. They are beyond help, and they are also in a minority. But those who know exactly what their fathers had done and say they oppose them, yet feel sorry for themselves because they have parents like that—I have no understanding for them. Nor for those who do not want to accept what they see or what has been pointed out to them.

Despite all the obstacles they face, I expect young Germans who want to become new democrats to break with their parents and confront them with the crucial question: Why did you do it?

A new German generation that does not question its parents would be the ideal matrix for a new fascism. In this instance love of parents, the cornerstone of civilized life, cannot be permitted to override all other considerations; it must almost turn into its opposite. For the children of Nazis the unconditional love of parents is an indulgence they cannot afford. History has condemned them to find out what their parents did, why they did it, and above all, why almost none of them ever felt guilt or shame after the war had ended. Only then can we believe that the Germans, the new Germans, are really different from their parents or grandparents.